The Complete Guide to
PATIOS

Updated 4th Edition

A DIY Guide to Building Patios, Walkways & Outdoor Steps

Quarto.com

© 2025 Quarto Publishing Group USA Inc.

Third edition published in 2014

Second edition published in 2010

First Published in 2007 by Cool Springs Press, an imprint of The Quarto Group, 100 Cummings Center, Suite 265-D, Beverly, MA 01915, USA. T (978) 282-9590 F (978) 283-2742

Cool Springs Press titles are also available at discount for retail, wholesale, promotional, and bulk purchase. For details, contact the Special Sales Manager by email at specialsales@quarto.com or by mail at The Quarto Group, Attn: Special Sales Manager, 100 Cummings Center, Suite 265-D, Beverly, MA 01915, USA.

29 28 27 26 25   1 2 3 4 5

ISBN: 978-0-7603-8890-7

Digital edition published in 2025
eISBN: 978-0-7603-8891-4

Originally found under the following LCCN: 2013039025

Cover Image: Shutterstock

Page Layout: *tabula rasa* graphic design

Illustration: Illustrations by Christopher Mills on pages 229 and 232
Illustrations by Ada Keesler on pages 182–183, 219–228, and 230–232, 234–235

Printed in China

BLACK+DECKER Complete Guide to Patios, 4th Edition

Created by: The Editors of Cool Springs Press, in cooperation with BLACK+DECKER.

BLACK+DECKER and the BLACK+DECKER logo are trademarks of The Black & Decker Corporation and are used under license. All rights reserved.

NOTICE TO READERS

For safety, use caution, care, and good judgment when following the procedures described in this book. The publisher and BLACK+DECKER cannot assume responsibility for any damage to property or injury to persons as a result of misuse of the information provided.

The techniques shown in this book are general techniques for various applications. In some instances, additional techniques not shown in this book may be required. Always follow manufacturers' instructions included with products, since deviating from the directions may void warranties. The projects in this book vary widely as to skill levels required: some may not be appropriate for all do-it-yourselfers, and some may require professional help.

Consult your local building department for information on building permits, codes, and other laws as they apply to your project.

Contents

INTRODUCTION	7

HARDSCAPING BASICS	9
Practical Considerations	10
Patio Design Gallery	16
Material Selection	24
Patio + Walkway Plans	34

PATIO PROJECTS	41
Layout + Surface Preparation	42
Patio Edging	48
Sandset Brick Patio	56
Cobblestone Paver Patio	63
Circular Paver Patio	70
Sandset Flagstone Patio	81
Concrete Slab Patio	88
Tiled Concrete Slab	96
Loose Materials Patio	104
Loose-fill Patio with Fire Pit	106

Contents (Cont.)

SPECIAL SECTION: NATURE-FRIENDLY PATIOS	**111**
Gallery of Nature-Friendly Patios	112
Creating a Permeable Subbase	116
Spaced Masonry Pavers	120
Composite Permeable Pavers	124
Rubber Tile Patio	128
Recycled Plastic Pavers	130
Subsurface Grids	133

WALKWAYS + STEPS	**137**
Designing Walkways + Steps	138
Sandset Brick Walkway	142
Poured Concrete Walkway	148
Decorative Concrete Path	154
Flagstone Walkway	158
Simple Gravel Path	161
Pebbled Stepping Stone Path	167
Timber Garden Steps	171
Flagstone Garden Steps	175
Low-Voltage Pathway + Patio Lighting	180

PATIO ROOMS + PROJECTS — **185**

Underdeck Patio — 186

Runoff Gutters — 193

Patio Enclosure — 196

Screened Patio Room — 210

Shade Sails — 218

Patio Kitchen — 222

Patio Bar — 228

A Patio Privacy-Screen Planter — 232

CONVERSION CHARTS — **236**

RESOURCES — **237**

PHOTOGRAPHY CREDITS — **238**

INDEX — **239**

Introduction

The evolution of the patio continues. Homeowners are no longer willing to settle for just a flat, level surface outside their back door. Where the patio was once and traditionally an afterthought hardscape transition to the yard and garden proper, it is now considered an extension of interior living space, with all the potential any room in the house holds.

That means that today's patio must provide a stable, eye-pleasing foundation seamlessly combining the comfort and luxury of a home's interior, with the joy and exposure of outdoor relaxation. The modern patio has, for all intents and purposes, become a true outdoor room and a stage for your aspirations.

Homeowners and designers are putting more and more thought into the surface underfoot, whether that surface is a patio, stairs, or even steps (or a combination of all three). Thankfully, they have a lot of options from which to choose. There have never been more potential patio materials available on the market. Each has its own unique look, attributes, and personality and they're all covered in this new, fourth edition of *BLACK+DECKER The Complete Guide to Patios*.

This updated version expands on the ways a patio can be visually tied to the home. You'll also find a lot more information on patio lighting possibilities, because the more patios become outdoor "rooms" the more homeowners want to enjoy them even at night, and perhaps every night.

The increased usage is why so many people are looking to equip their outdoor stage with fully featured, weather-resistant outdoor kitchens and fireplaces. The average run-of-the mill patio grill is no longer the goal. These days, it's all about complete gas cooktops with refined controls and other specialty features like pizza ovens. Firepits are still a favorite, but homeowners with space and a bit more ambition now often opt for a full-blown fireplace with chimney. It doesn't hurt that a showstopping built-in patio feature adds to property value.

Another growing trend in modern patio design is toward an increasing sense of drama. Many homeowners look to actually create "walls" for their outdoor rooms, courtesy of beautiful fabric drapes that can be raised or lower as the mood dictates. You can even create a sun-blocking ceiling overhead, with a colorful shade sail, or fabric panels threaded artfully between the rafters of an arbor. Other potential overhangs include a wide range of house-mounted awnings. Privacy screens are also on the rise, because they create more discreet, cozy, and unique outdoor entertaining areas. They are also an easy way to accent the patio's design.

Throw in all the plants you can add around the edges of a patio for a greater visual impact and lovely aroma and the question isn't whether you should add a patio to your home, it's what size and type you should opt for. The answer lies in the pages of this book.

Hardscaping Basics

The main difference between patios (and the walkways and steps that serve those surfaces) and decks is the surface used underfoot. While decks are usually limited to wood or composites, patios have far fewer limitations. That opens the door to an amazing range of creative possibilities.

This chapter begins by exploring those options, with stunning pictures that should serve as creative inspiration. Not only will you discover an eye-opening diversity of patio surfaces, you'll also find examples of patio themes that are gracing yards large and small. The lesson is this: There is simply no excuse for a boring patio.

That said, there are certainly practical considerations that must go into the design of your patio. Those are amply covered in this chapter, as well. They include the best material choices for the location, ideal siting to avoid wind alleys or sunblasted surfaces, ideal shapes and sizes, zoning restrictions, and ensuring proper drainage.

Finally, you can consult the site plans included here as food for thought in drafting your own. Just as a floorplan is essential to building a room addition, a site plan—even a rough, hand-drawn sketch—is key to creating the patio of your dreams.

In This Chapter:

- Material Selection
- Practical Considerations
- Patio & Walkway Plans

Practical Considerations

In addition to the creative work of planning the look and feel of a patio space, there are several practical matters that must be addressed before you can hit the drawing board. Thinking about how you will use the patio will help you answer one of the biggest questions—how much space you'll need. The planning stage is also the time to consider environmental factors, including site drainage, sunlight, and wind, to make sure your patio will be both comfortable and usable whenever you're ready to get outside. Finally, check with your city's building department to learn about building code requirements and zoning restrictions that might affect your project plans.

Use

No matter how beautiful the surface may be, the measure of any patio is how well it helps you, your family and friends enjoy your home's outdoor spaces. What will be the primary uses for the space? Dining, entertaining, sunbathing, playing with the kids, enjoying the view? Once you establish the uses, figure out how you can accommodate all of those activities within an attractive, efficient design. For some, the solution lies simply in providing adequate space in a flexible floor plan—a quick shift in furniture, for example, can set the stage for the next activity.

Imagine the ideal setup for each activity. For example, if you have young children, maybe you want a comfortable sitting area near an edge of the patio that's adjacent to a sandbox (or even a sandbox built into the patio; when the youngest has outgrown it, you can turn it into a planting bed). Or maybe you want some space on the patio for a baby pool or a fountain for the kids to play in.

A patio that's good for entertaining, as well as everyday uses, requires a balanced plan. Large, open areas are best for hosting parties, but can feel empty and overly exposed for a small group of diners. To accommodate both, separate expansive areas from more intimate spaces with a change in floor level or create a more personal, sheltered space by tucking a furniture set into a corner under an arbor. And don't

VISUALIZING YOUR PATIO

Create a quick mock-up to help you plan your patio's size, shape, and location. Mark the proposed space with rope or garden hose, and set out any furniture you'll use. See how it all looks from different points on your lot, as well as from inside the house.

forget to include some personal space: the perfect spot where your favorite chair is always ready for a little reading time or a quick snooze.

Size & Layout

The ideal size and configuration for your patio is determined by the space needed for each activity, including plenty of room for easy access and traffic flow. With the floor space allocated, you can begin playing around with different layouts, design elements, and shapes until the form of the space accommodates all of its functions. All the while, keep the big picture in mind—make sure the proportions and general design of the patio complement your house and the rest of the landscape.

How Much Space?

If you already have the patio furniture, set it up on the proposed site and experiment with different arrangements to get a sense of how much space each furniture grouping will need. If you don't have the furniture yet, see the illustration below for suggestions on spacing.

Next, decide which areas you want to dedicate to specific activities and which can be rearranged for multiple uses. Cooking and dining areas are best as static, or *anchored*, stations, while an informal sunbathing spot defined by a couple of lounge chairs can easily be rearranged or moved as needed.

To plan traffic routes, allow a minimum of 22 inches of width for main passages between and alongside activity areas (32 inches minimum for wheelchair access). The main goal is having enough room for traffic to smoothly flow around the patio.

Design Factors

No patio is designed in isolation. Consider carefully how the patio's scale, style, and materials look in relation to the house and surrounding structures. Does the surface accommodate all you want to do? Is it oriented to take advantage of the best view, and how will it interact or relate to existing landscape,

or any plantings you will add? Are there features, such as an arbor, privacy screen, or stone wall that will improve and integrate the patio design into its surroundings?

Nestling this poolside social area into the wooded property border softens the hard lines and unforgiving textures of the poured concrete forms, and creates a sense of intimacy and comfort that the patio would not have had if it had been placed at the end of the pool.

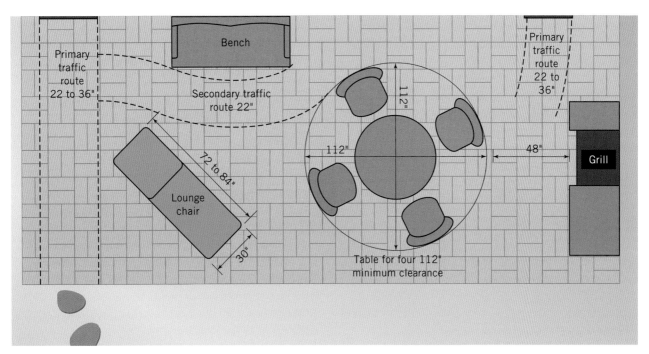

When arranging your patio, consider the placement of furniture and permanent structures as well as the space needed for primary traffic routes. These routes should have a minimum width of 22" to allow for comfortable passage throughout the patio.

Contact local utility companies to have all utility lines marked on your property. This is necessary before digging in your yard, and it could affect your patio location. Utility companies promptly send out a representative to mark the lines.

Zoning Laws, Building Codes, & Utilities

Any alterations made to your lot could fall under your municipality's zoning laws. In the case of a new patio, zoning laws might limit locations for the patio and how much ground it can cover. The latter relates to the allowable percentage of development on the lot (adding a large patio now could preclude future plans for a home addition).

Also make sure the patio conforms to setback restrictions (required distance from lot lines) and easements (zones that must be accessible for utilities and other public services). Walls, fire features, or overhead structures may be subject to standards set by the local building codes, and you may need to obtain building permits.

Discuss your plans with the local building or zoning department. If you run into snags, ask about alternatives; for example, a poured concrete patio may not be allowed over an easement, but a less permanent, sandset surface may be approved.

Also, contact the local utility companies to have underground utility lines marked on your property.

Access

Like most recreation and relaxation areas, a patio tends to be used more often if it's easily accessible. The same is true of visual access. Full views, or even just glimpses, of the patio from several interior rooms will beckon you outdoors on nice days.

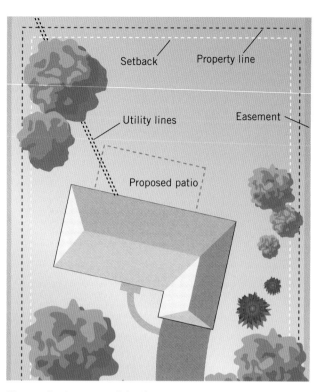

Always check your municipality's zoning laws when planning a new patio project.

Another important consideration involves the rooms that lead to the patio. For example, if outdoor dining is one of your primary activities, locating the patio near the kitchen will prove to be an enormous convenience. Similarly, a patio used frequently for large parties should not be accessed through a bedroom or other private space. This is an inconvenience, and guests feel uncomfortable walking through private or formal areas of a home.

Atmosphere

It's easy to overlook the environmental elements that will impact how enjoyable your patio will be. For instance, sun exposure may lead you to reposition a patio under a shade tree or plan for a shade sail or large umbrella. If wind is an issue, you may need to create some sort of artificial wind break with a fence or potted plants. Noise from a nearby street may mean modifying the plans to include a sound-dampening privacy screen. The point is to carefully consider all ambient elements that are directly related to the patio's construction, but that could impact your time spent in the outdoor area.

Dealing with Drainage

It's not unusual that a new patio creates, or is subject to, drainage problems. One common cause is a hard paved surface that sheds water instead of absorbing it and deposits it along the lower edge of the patio. There, the water collects, creating a swampy area of grass.

During heavy rains, runoff water can build up enough force to wash out flower beds bordering a patio. Drainage problems can also occur when the water has no escape, a common condition with sunken or recessed patios that are surrounded by retaining walls or ascending slopes. Adding or removing soil or plants to make room for a patio can alter natural drainage patterns, potentially resulting in an unpleasant surprise with the first good rain.

Fortunately, all of these problems can be solved with an appropriate drainage system. For patio runoff, a drainage swale or perimeter trench is usually effective. These are sloped channels or trenches that collect excess groundwater and divert it to a collection point. A trench running along the lowest edge of the patio can collect water directly from the patio surface. If the patio is at the top of a natural slope leading to a low point in the yard, a drainage swale located in the low point keeps the rest of the yard relatively dry.

Diverting excess water is only half of the battle—the water also needs a place to go. Ideally, it is collected on your property, where it filters through the soil and returns to natural aquifers. This can be achieved with a dry well or with a swale leading to a natural collection area in the landscape. Another option is to divert excess runoff to a street gutter or a storm drain, but this design must be approved by the city's planning department. For further discussion on surface drainage and environmental considerations, see page 33.

Enclosed or recessed patios may require their own drainage system, typically with some type of floor drain. The patio surface slopes toward the drain, located either in the center or along one side, where runoff water collects in a subsurface catch basin. From there, an underground drainpipe carries the water to a collection point.

If you think your patio will need this type of system, consult an engineer or qualified landscape professional early in the planning process to discuss your options.

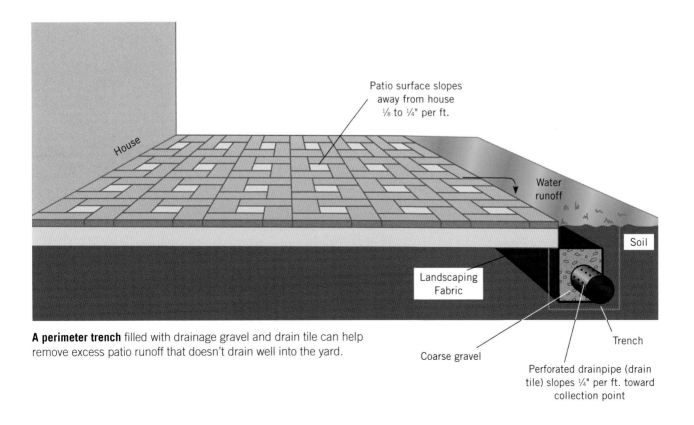

Patio surface slopes away from house ⅛ to ¼" per ft.

House

Water runoff

Soil

Landscaping Fabric

Coarse gravel

Trench

Perforated drainpipe (drain tile) slopes ¼" per ft. toward collection point

A perimeter trench filled with drainage gravel and drain tile can help remove excess patio runoff that doesn't drain well into the yard.

Climate Control

Careful planning can't change the weather, but it can help you make the best of prevailing conditions. By controlling exposure to sunlight and shade, wind, and natural air currents, you can make your patio the most comfortable place in your outdoor landscape. Consider the following:

Sunlight and shadows: The unalterable pattern of the sun is one of the few climatic systems you can count on. The tricky part is positioning your patio so it receives the right amount and intensity of sunlight at the time of day—and the season—when you'll use it most. Remember that the sun's path changes throughout the year. In summer, it rises high in the sky along the east-west axis, creating shorter shadows and more exposure overall. In winter, the sun's angle is relatively low, resulting in long shadows in the northwest, north, and northeast directions. To avoid shadows altogether, locate your patio away from the house and other structures.

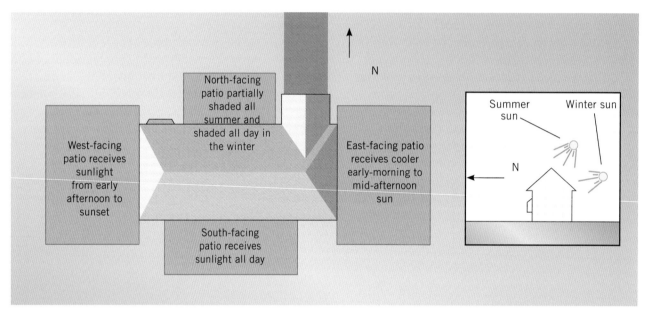

Sun exposure changes throughout the day and from season to season. You can use any of several sun-mapping smartphone apps to track the sun's path at your specific location.

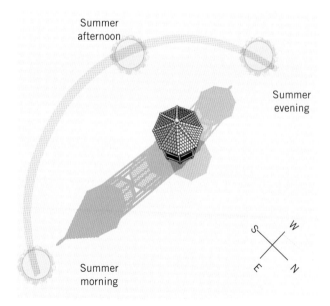

Shadows follow the east-west axis in the summer.

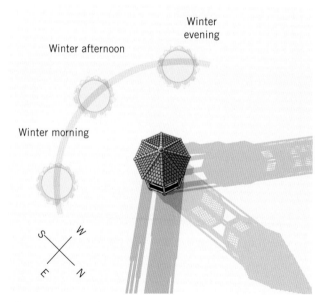

Winter shadows point to the northeast and northwest and are relatively long at midday.

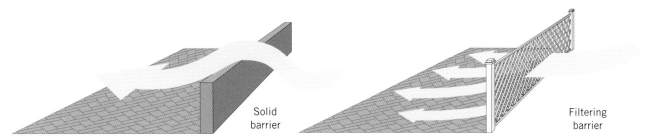

Barriers help control wind patterns around your patio. Solid barriers drive wind currents upward, creating a forcible reversal in direction. Filtering barriers allow wind to pass through, reducing its force in the process.

Wind currents can ruin your patio peace as surely as a rainstorm. Shielding yourself from wind takes careful planning and sometimes trial and error. Since you can't protect against all wind, first determine the direction of prevailing winds—the most frequent and strongest wind currents affecting your site (prevailing winds may change with the seasons)—then decide on the best location for a wind barrier.

Contrary to appearances, a solid barrier often is not the most effective windbreak; these barriers force air currents to swoop over the top and then drop down on the backside, returning to full strength at a distance roughly equal to the barrier's height. A more reliable windbreak is created with a lattice or louvered fence that diffuses and weakens the wind as it passes through the barrier.

Patio materials and orientation: The surface material you choose can also affect the patio environment. Dark-colored, solid surfaces—like brick or dark stone—absorb a lot of heat during the day and may become uncomfortable to walk on in sunny areas. However, after the sun goes down, stored heat released from the paving can warm the air on the patio. Solid walls also reflect heat and can restrict cooling breezes. Because cold air sinks, low-lying patios or those positioned at the base of an incline tend to be cooler than higher areas of the landscape.

If you're building an overhead specifically for shade, experiment with alternative materials, such as bamboo screening or fabric, to filter sunlight and control wind.

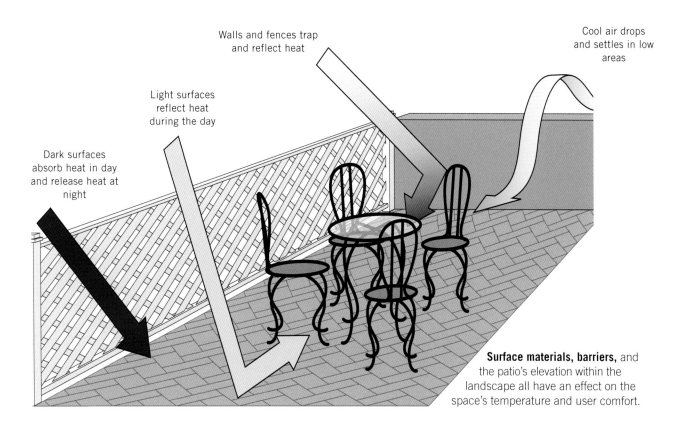

Walls and fences trap and reflect heat

Cool air drops and settles in low areas

Light surfaces reflect heat during the day

Dark surfaces absorb heat in day and release heat at night

Surface materials, barriers, and the patio's elevation within the landscape all have an effect on the space's temperature and user comfort.

Patio Design Gallery

Most patio designs start out based on function. That might be as simple as a stable surface on which to set a dining table so it won't rock, or to reserve a bit of hardscape where you can sunbathe or simply relax and unwind. Patio looks, however, can go far beyond function. No matter what the purpose the surface is intended for, it can easily be embellished with additional features that help it stand out, or even blend into its surroundings. This gallery offers prime examples of successful designs that not only accommodate common outdoor uses, but also look fantastic in their own right.

Alfresco at Home

Surround your dining patio with lush landscaping to create a beautiful place to dine and a sense of privacy, mystery, and romance. The plantings around this modest patio include both flowering and foliage plants, providing visual interest year round and a constantly changing backdrop to the outdoor dining room.

Magnify modern style with a monochrome look. A stunning patio surface made of mottled, preformed concrete pavers adds tons of linear design interest while blending perfectly with the sophisticated gray concrete walls of this modern home. A luxury overhead infrared heater makes this patio dining alcove usable even on cool nights and over four seasons.

Up the comfort with a custom firepit. A firepit built to match the patio provides the perfect social center in this mortared stone patio. A drinks ledge adds functionality, and the size of the firepit ensures that it kicks of plentiful heat for chilly cocktail hours and colder days. Luxury patio chairs make this pleasant patio corner even more comfortable.

Overhead Structures

Exploit an arbor for maximum flexibility. An arbor like this one provides excellent support for plants—hanging or climbing—and adds an interesting overhead visual that still allows for a view through to the day or night sky. The structure is also handy for additions like a cooling fan and can even be a frame for sun-blocking fabric panels.

Let the landscape shine. This simple concrete patio—laid and scored in a linear grid—is the ideal stage for understated but upscale outdoor chairs and adjustable umbrella. The wild, natural surroundings serve as the perfect backdrop and provide an endlessly enjoyable visual feast from the patio.

Add an overhang to double the fun. This luxury patio benefits from a house-attached overhang that provides a comfy, protected sitting area, while leaving the rest of the patio—and a decorative, centerpiece fountain—uncovered.

Focus on Fire

Let the firepit be the star. A stunning, sleek, modern house is well-complemented by a simple poured-concrete patio. A showpiece firepit does justice to both, putting an enchanting outdoor gathering area mere feet from the back door.

Light for drama as well as safety. This stand-alone concrete patio, with integral pillars and roof, dominates the yard at night as much as during the day, thanks to uplights at the base of each roof pillar. Matching uplighting is used to great effect to show off the wall of hedges. Notice how the concrete pavers across the lawn perfectly complement the patio.

Mix and match naturally compatible materials. Here, oversized sandstone pavers are paired with a natural wood built-in bench, a stone firepit, and a stacked stone background wall. The mixture of textures and shapes provides a wealth of dynamic visual interest, but all the different surfaces are tied together as natural materials that might be found next to one another in nature itself.

Add task lighting for safety. Dramatic uplights or soft, diffuse walkway LEDs can be lovely, but where you'll be working with knives and food, strong lighting is a must. The illumination in this outdoor kitchen is appropriately boosted with undercounter LED lighting strips that make it attractive and completely usable, even at night.

Pool Partners

Go modern with crisp lines and bold solid colors. This modest backyard is turned into a showcase of stunning modern style thanks to a linear set of concrete patios, with blocky, squared-off furniture. The overhang structure is painted an eye-catching black, and the linear nature of the entire look is clean, sharp, and attractive.

Repeat patterns to blend patio and pool. The sharp, stuccoed surface and expansion lines that define the pool apron have been replicated in this adjacent patio. Although the patio dining area is separated from the pool by a strip of grass, the entire yard appears as one coordinated and integrated design.

Keep function in mind when designing a pool patio. The mix of concrete and pavers that form this pool patio add undeniable visual interest to the area, but they are also both slip-resistant surfaces that can absorb water and prevent falls. All patio design should be thoughtful, but never more so than where safety is an issue.

Material Selection

Brick, stone, and concrete rightly make up most people's short list of good patio and walkway surfaces, but these materials in their basic forms are just the beginning. Brick alone comes in a range of colors, textures, and styles, while the availability of stone and the variety of concrete pavers are both constantly expanding. After giving some thought to your preferred patio surface, it will be well worth it to spend a few hours browsing local stone yards, landscape suppliers, and building centers to see what's available in your area. Ask about delivery pricing while you're there.

Brick

Natural clay brick is generally considered a classic surface material for patios and walkways—a well-deserved distinction. With its combination of warm, natural coloring and texture and its orderly geometric shapes, brick is the perfect blend of house and garden. And with its small unit size, brick is also quite versatile and can be easily applied to formal layouts or imaginative curved patterns. The standard brick patio installation consists of setting brick into a sand bed in an ordered pattern, but brick can also be mortared over a concrete patio slab or walkway for a highly finished appearance and a surface that won't be affected by ground movement.

Bricks for outdoor surfaces are called pavers. These flat, solid units have a porous texture that helps provide traction in wet weather. Brick dimensions vary by manufacturer and range approximately from $1\frac{1}{8}$ to $2\frac{3}{4}$ inches in thickness. The standard size (width and length) for sandset (mortarless) installation is 4×8 inches. Bricks for mortared jobs are a little smaller to account for the mortar joints.

Pavers are also rated for load-bearing strength and weather resistance. Types 2 and 3 are suitable for heavy foot traffic. SX (or SW) brick is for cold climates, MX brick is for warm climates without a hard frost, and NX brick is for interior applications. Don't use standard wall brick, fire brick, or other types of building brick for flooring surfaces.

Brick is a classic patio and walkway paving material. A wide variety of looks are available at reasonable prices, the size is standardized, and bricks are easy to work with and design into even a complicated pattern, such as the formal herringbone of this walkway

Concrete Pavers

Concrete pavers are the most popular alternative to traditional brick and are installed the same way—either sandset or mortared over a concrete slab. Like brick, concrete pavers are highly durable, and their uniform dimensions make them easy to work with. While most clay bricks only come in standard rectangular units, concrete pavers are available in a wide range of sizes and shapes, including small and large rectangles and squares, various interlocking designs, and trapezoidal shapes used for circular and fan patterns.

Concrete pavers can be manufactured with different textures and edge treatments that can greatly alter their appearance. Among the most popular styles are "tumbled" pavers that have softened, randomly chipped edges, giving the paving an age-worn look. The tumbled effect is an important component of the many cobblestone styles of concrete paving.

For sandset installations, you can use virtually any type of concrete paver. Many come with spacing lugs molded into the sides of each unit—these automatically set an even space between pavers that you fill with sand to complete the installation (most clay bricks don't have spacing lugs, and you have to set the gaps with temporary spacers). For mortared finishes, choose concrete pavers with square sides (with or without spacing lugs); interlocking styles and other irregular shapes make it difficult to fill and finish the mortar joints.

Concrete paver products have evolved from commercial-looking units in basic pink and tan tones to a diverse assortment of colors, shapes, and textures. Pavers are now commonly available in sets of blended colors and shapes for a more natural look; they are tumbled with nicely variegated patterns.

Stone

Natural stone has an organic beauty that's unmatched by all other building materials. Stone paving is used all over the world in grand courtyards, ancient roadways, and backyard landscapes alike. In nature, stones frequently form paths for crossing streams and skirting muddy fields—it's not surprising, then, that it's a popular material for patios and walkways.

Flagstone

Flagstone is the general term given to any broad, flat stone that has been split to a thickness of around one to four inches, making it good for paving. Common species of flagstone include sandstone, limestone, bluestone, and slate. Individual stones may have cut edges for paving in linear patterns, while stones with jagged edges and irregular shapes are best for creating a patio or walkway surface with a natural, casual feel.

Flagstones can be set in sand or stable (tamped) soil, or they can be permanently laid in mortar over a concrete patio slab or walkway. For an organic, stepping-stone effect, you can space stones widely and fill the gaps with gravel or groundcover plantings.

Availability of flagstone varies by region; see what types are offered at local stone yards. For paving on patios and primary walkways, make sure the stone is thick enough for furniture and/or heavy foot traffic and that the surface of the stones won't become dangerously slick when wet.

Natural flagstone is cleft into slabs with irregular shapes and an often interesting, flaky top surface. Flagstone is also available in precut tiles.

The beauty, strength, and unique character of stone makes it a natural choice for all sorts of hardscaping, especially patios, walkways, and garden paths. Paving a path with stones of varying shapes and sizes is just one way to create a one-of-a-kind paving surface.

Stone Tile

Many types of stone can be cut into flat, square, or rectangular tiles for outdoor paving. Slate, granite, marble, limestone, and quartzite are among the most common species of stone tile. In contrast to uncut flagstone's natural variation in thickness, shape, and texture, stone tile is more uniform and closer in appearance to manufactured tile. Its visual effect is a nice combination of natural texture and coloring with orderly geometric patterns.

Most stone tile is too thin to support foot traffic when laid over a soft base and must be installed in mortar over a concrete slab. For thicker tiles and stronger species of stone suitable for sandset paving, check with local suppliers. It's important to discuss your plans with your tile supplier, as not all tiles are suitable for all applications, especially outdoors. A local tile dealer will know what works best in your local climate.

BUYING STONE

Paving stone is typically sold by the square yard or by the ton. Before you start shopping, calculate the area of your patio in square feet. Stone suppliers can use this number to estimate your requirements in tons, if necessary. Buying in bulk from a stone yard is less expensive than hand-selecting individual stones, though you don't get to inspect all of the pieces in advance. Also, purchasing bulk shipments preloaded onto pallets helps prevent breakage before and during delivery. To estimate quantities of stone tile, calculate the total area you need to cover, then factor in the thickness of the grout joints. Your tile supplier can help with these calculations.

Here are some other things to think about when considering stone for your patio or walkway:

- In general, the difficulty of quarrying and dressing stone makes it a relatively expensive material. The more work that's done to the raw material—hand-selection, cutting, and finishing—the higher the cost.

- When it comes to a finished patio, one of the main drawbacks of some flagstone is its uneven surface, which can lead to wobbly tables and the occasional stubbed toe. However, many people choose stone specifically for its natural "imperfections."

- Softer flagstone, such as sandstone, can split fairly easily if not supported evenly from below. Sandstone is also vulnerable to scratches from shovels, chair legs, and other metal objects.

- Slate and some other types of flagstone and tile can be slippery when wet—an important consideration for exposed surfaces.

At the other end of the spectrum from irregular, cleft flagstone, stone tile surfaces are orderly and refined. Yet, even with precise, formal patterns like this, the natural coloring of stone adds an organic quality that you don't get with most manufactured tile.

Poured Concrete

The patios and walkways of most new homes today are poured concrete. Concrete is the default outdoor surface for several reasons: it's the cheapest of the hardscape materials, it's extremely durable and virtually maintenance free, and it involves the quickest installation (especially for a professional concrete crew). Also, if the homeowners don't like the look of bare concrete, it can always be covered with another outdoor material or stained to add a permanent touch of color.

The same benefits hold true for a do-it-yourselfer building a new concrete patio or walkway. While a big concrete pour is a challenging undertaking for amateurs, a walkway or even a small patio is certainly a doable project. The secret to success is to take the time to prepare the site properly, stake your forms well, and watch the wet concrete carefully as it sets up so you'll know when to begin the finishing steps.

For first-timers, it's always a good idea to start with something small, such as a walkway or small utility slab, to learn the overall process and the nuances of finishing concrete before you tackle a bigger project.

A poured concrete slab or walkway can be a finished surface by itself, or it can serve as the structural foundation for other surface materials, including mortared brick and concrete pavers, stone, and tile. In fact, mortared finishes must be laid over a stable concrete foundation—soil or even compacted gravel may cause the mortar to crack. Whether you're leaving the concrete bare or you're planning to cover it with a mortared-in material, the basic construction steps are the same, though a bare concrete slab requires a little more finishing to ensure a smooth surface. Another popular use of poured concrete is pouring walkways with concrete molds, as shown on page 29.

A poured concrete patio is the perfect poolside surface. Slip proof, chic, and a great foil for the blue water feature, this surface also blends well with the modern home, upscale dining set, and adaptable cantilevered umbrella.

Decorative Effects

While many people like the clean, monolithic look of a plain concrete slab, there are several options for adding decorative touches to a new concrete surface:

Seeded concrete is finished with a layer of fine stones for a uniform, yet organic, effect. This is a popular choice for patios because of its multicolored, textured appearance and nonslip surface.

A divided concrete slab is poured with permanent wood dividers and border edging, separating the slab into equal sections. In addition to its decorative value, a divided slab is also easier to work with, since it allows you to pour and finish one section at a time, if desired.

Tinting and acid staining introduce a range of color options to the familiar cement gray of plain concrete. Commercial colorants, available in both liquid and powdered forms, can be added to wet concrete mix for consistent color throughout the material. This is a good option for mold-formed walkways and other projects that call for small batches of wet concrete. For larger projects, you can order ready-mix concrete in a limited range of colors. Acid staining is a simple, permanent treatment for cured concrete slabs and can be applied at any time after the concrete has fully cured.

One of the best things about poured concrete is its malleability: in its liquid form, concrete follows curves and angles just as well as straight lines, making it a great medium for custom shapes and sizes.

Walkway molds are filled with poured concrete for easy path or patio construction. The finished product has the appearance of a continuous surface but does not have the same structural properties of a solid concrete walkway.

Loose Materials

Loose materials for patios and walkways encompass a wide range of natural elements, from gravel to wood chips to small river stones. You can use a loose material by itself to create a simple patio or path surface, or use it as infill between an arrangement of heavier materials, such as flagstone or large,

Loose materials can work well on their own or as a complement to surrounding elements. In this landscape, buff-colored gravel serves as both a primary surface and an infill material for a stepping stone path. The natural look of the gravel provides a nice contrast to the formal paver walkway and patio.

concrete stepping pavers. In contrast to the solidity and permanence of traditional paving, loose materials have a casual, summery feel. Walking over a pathway of crushed stone or wood chips can feel like a stroll down a country lane or a walk through the woods.

As a primary surface, loose materials offer several practical advantages. They drain well, are forgiving of uneven ground, and can be replenished and graded with a rake for a quick facelift. They also tend to be much less expensive than most other paving options and couldn't be easier to install. Start with a bed of compacted gravel and cover it with landscape fabric to inhibit weed growth and separate the gravel base from the surface material. Then, spread out the material a few inches thick, compact it if necessary, and you're done!

For simpler applications, such as a lightly traveled garden path, you can often skip the gravel base and lay the landscape fabric right over leveled and tamped soil. In most cases, it's best to include a raised edging to contain the material and maintain the shape of the paved surface.

Selecting Loose Materials

Because different loose materials can have very different textures and properties, it's important to choose the right surface for the application. Here's a look at some of the most popular materials for patios and walkways:

Decomposed granite: A popular choice for level patios, paths, and driveways, decomposed granite (DG) can be compacted to a relatively smooth, flat, hard surface. DG consists of small pieces of granite ranging in size from sand-size grains to a quarter inch. The variation is the reason this material is so compactable. DG is available in various natural shades of gray, brown, and tan. Due to its gritty, sandy finish that can stick to your shoes, DG is not a good choice for surfaces that receive heavy traffic directly to and from the house.

Pea gravel and crushed stone: Pea gravel and crushed stone include a broad range of gravel, from fine textures to very coarse. Pea gravel is small- to medium-sized stone that is either mechanically crushed or shaped naturally by water. Crushed stone typically consists of coarse, jagged pieces in various sizes, generally larger than pea gravel. Many types of gravel are compactable, but usually less so than DG.

Decomposed granite

Pea gravel

Crushed stone

Gravel made up of round stones is more comfortable to walk on than jagged materials.

River rock: Smoothed and rounded by water or machines, river rock ranges from small stones to baseball-sized (and larger) rocks. These smooth surfaces make it more comfortable to walk on than jagged gravel but it is also less compactable and easily displaced underfoot. Larger stones are difficult to walk on and are more suitable for accent areas than for primary paving surfaces.

Wood chips: Wood chips and mulch are commonly used as groundcover in planting beds, gardens, and flowerbeds. Most types are soft and springy underfoot, and many can be used for light-traffic paths and even children's play areas. Wood chips come in a wide variety of grades, colors, and textures. In general, finely chopped and consistent materials are more expensive and more formal in appearance than coarse blends. The term *mulch* is often used interchangeably with wood chips but can also describe roughly chopped wood and other organic matter that's best suited for beds and ground cover. Most loose material made of wood needs some replenishing every two to four years.

Both stone and wood loose materials are typically sold in bulk at landscape and garden centers and by the bag at home centers. Buying in bulk is often much less expensive for all but the smallest jobs. Landscape and garden suppliers typically offer bulk deliveries for a reasonable flat fee. Due to the variance in terminology and appearance of loose materials, be sure to visit the supplier and take a look at the materials you're buying firsthand, so you know exactly what to expect.

River rock

Wood chips

Tile

With its neat, geometric lines and smooth finish, manufactured tile is a great choice for a formal patio or a nicely appointed front entry. In warm climates, tile is a common outdoor material, often seen in courtyards and fountain plazas paved with large, handmade earthen tiles. In colder regions, outdoor tile must be nearly impervious to water to withstand winter's freeze-thaw cycles. Tile should always be installed over a concrete slab. In fact, this is one of its main uses—the thin profile of most tile makes it a good material for covering a drab, old concrete surface with a fresh, new finish.

Selecting Tile

Indoors, you can use just about any kind of floor tile, but patios are a different matter. Patio tile must be strong enough to survive scrapes from outdoor furniture as well as years of weather and sun exposure. More importantly, patio tile must be slip-resistant, which automatically rules out most glazed tile. The main types of tile suitable for outdoor use are quarry, terra-cotta, and porcelain, in addition to natural stone (see page 24).

Quarry tile is a durable ceramic tile that comes unglazed in many colors. It often has a flat but slightly abrasive surface for good slip-resistance.

Terra-cotta tile has a warm, natural appearance, usually in mottled earth tones. It looks great on patios, but because it is somewhat porous, it is not recommended for use in cold climates.

Saltillo tile is a dried, rather than fired, tile similar to terra-cotta but with a more imperfect, handmade character. It is also only suitable for mild climates.

Porcelain tile is the toughest, hardest, and often most expensive manufactured tile you can buy. It is highly resistant to water and therefore a good choice for patios in most climates.

When shopping for outdoor tile, be sure to discuss your plans with knowledgeable sales staff. A good tile dealer can help you choose the right type and style of tile for your application and the local climate. They can also help you select appropriate grout and provide maintenance tips for keeping your patio surface in shape throughout the years. Be aware that some tile can discolor or fade over time, due to sun exposure. Sealing grout and, in some cases, tile surfaces are often recommended to prevent staining and to prolong the life of the installation; ask your tile dealer for recommendations.

Tile adds a highly finished look to a patio floor—perfect for an outdoor room with an indoor feel. Like standard floor tile, patio tiles are set into a mortar bed (over a flat concrete slab); then are grouted to complete the job.

Environmentally-friendly Materials

One way to go green is to choose patio paving materials made with recycled components or to use reclaimed materials, such as salvaged brick, reclaimed timbers, or chunks of old concrete. It's also smart to consider how your patio will shed runoff water and how that might affect local flooding zones and waterways.

There are many different options for recycled paving, as well as edging and other landscaping materials. For loose material paving and infill applications, you can buy recycled crushed brick in a range of textures. Pavers made from recycled glass are available in several standard sizes for general paving and in large stepping stone sizes. For concrete pavers, look for products made with recycled glass aggregate. Recycled rubber is used in a number of different products, including "paver" patio mats and granulated mulch for loose-fill applications and play areas. If you're looking for eco-friendly edging for a patio or path, consider flexible edging and landscape timbers made from recycled plastic.

Loose infill can be some of the most environmentally responsible material you can use for patios and pathways. The crushed rock here is an example of a fast-draining, ecological option. As a bonus, it looks wonderful lit up at night by a stylish, decorative fixture.

Using salvaged brick for patios, walkways, or edging is a good application for reusing materials. This yard also forgoes grass for mulch, which saves on water use. The yard is still a lush green due to the hardy vines and low-maintenance shrubs. Note: Not all salvaged brick is suitable for primary paving surfaces. When setting brick in mortar, be sure to use compatible mortar to prevent cracking.

Permeable paving is an important element of green landscape design for the simple reason that it allows storm water to filter into the ground instead of flowing into municipal drainage systems, where it contributes to flooding problems and contamination of local waterways. Permeable patio and walkway surfaces include sandset pavers and stone, as well as all loose materials, while poured concrete and mortared surfaces are essentially impermeable.

From a green standpoint, impermeable surfaces are fine as long as your patio or walkway is sloped toward an area of natural ground that is large enough to capture and absorb all (or most) seasonal runoff. However, if you have a large paved surface that drains onto another impermeable surface, such as a driveway or street, consider using a permeable paving material instead of solid concrete, or plan for an adequate buffer zone of natural ground between the new surface and other paved areas.

Patio + Walkway Plans

This section offers a different kind of inspiration from the section on design. Here you'll see detailed patio and landscape plans for several different types of properties, each showing specific design solutions for making the most of the available space and existing conditions. One or more of the properties might resemble your own, but even if none of them does, don't worry; the idea is to see how various elements can be put to use and to think about how some of those solutions might work in your own plan.

The five designs, starting on the following page, are shown in *plan*, or aerial, view. This is the perspective that professionals use to do much of their design work, as it provides not only a bird's-eye view of the entire site, it's also the best way to see how the patio, walkways, and other elements relate to the house and surrounding landscape. Plan drawings of your own property can be quite helpful in designing and planning a new patio or path project (see below).

 ## DRAWING YOUR OWN PLANS

Unless you need them for getting a permit or other official business, detailed drawings of your site and new projects are optional. But there are a few good reasons to map out your property and at least sketch your basic plans onto paper. Scaled drawings are good for showing relationships between elements and overall proportions within a plan, and are helpful for estimating materials and making shopping lists. If you hire out any of the work, detailed drawings will be invaluable for obtaining accurate bids and to help you keep the project on track during construction. Also, sketches are always useful for conveying or experimenting with ideas.

When making your own drawings, it's best to work from a base map, or site plan—an aerial view of the project site and as much of the surrounding area as is relevant. The site plan should include:

- The house (at least the wall adjacent to the patio), including doors, windows, and light fixtures
- Trees, significant plantings, and other landscaping features
- Gutter downspouts, outdoor faucets, and electrical outlets
- Notes about prevailing winds, lot grading (for sloping sites), and natural drainage routes
- Views (good and bad) from the patio site
- Sun and wind patterns

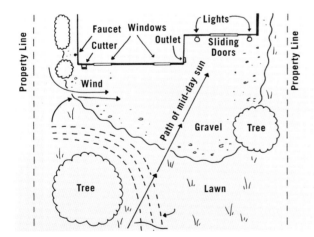

An accurately scaled site plan puts your property into perspective and helps you think like a designer. Create a plan using your own measurements or locate the plat map or original blueprints of your property (check with the local city or county planning offices or your mortgage company).

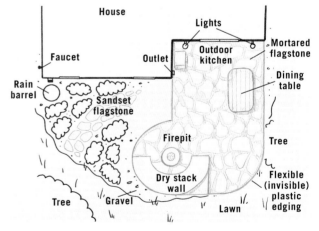

Sketch your designs onto clean copies of the site plan, or use an overlay of tracing paper for each new drawing. As you refine your plans, create more detailed, smaller-scale drawings of the patio/walkway site and immediate surroundings.

Sample Patio Plan 1

Like most lots in established urban neighborhoods, this backyard space was short on both space and privacy. But by devoting most of the area to two patios and the rest to planting beds, this design provides ample room for entertaining, outdoor dining, and even gardening.

The main patio space is paved with cut stone for a natural yet clean look and a smooth surface that's good for nighttime parties and frequent traffic between the house and the back gate. In one corner, a flagstone coffee table and fountain define a casual "lounge" area; the fountain also helps dampen the city's noise. A vine-covered arbor (or trellis) provides shade and privacy for half of the lounge area and a portion of the smaller planting bed.

Opposite the lounge area, a cozy corner patio is the perfect stage for intimate gatherings and everyday meals. Its natural flagstone floor is two short steps up from the main patio surface. This, along with the decorative post-and-beam gate, gives the dining space a special, secluded feel. A fan-shaped arbor could be added here for shade and more privacy.

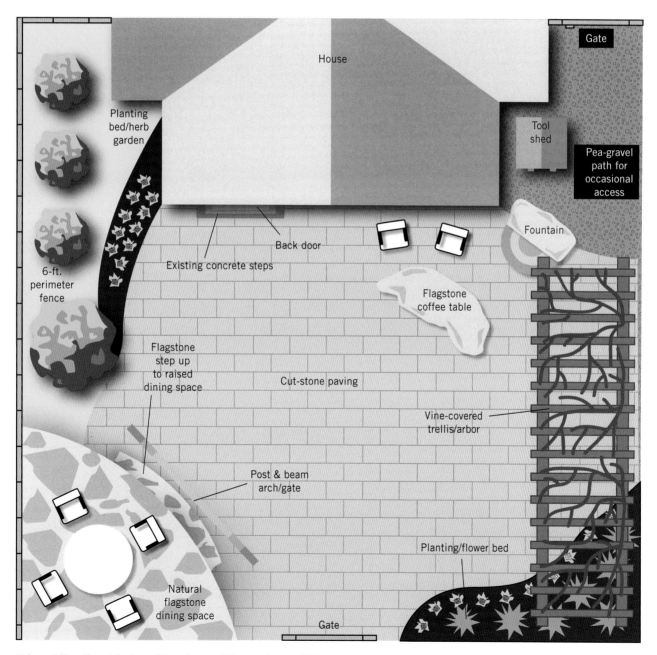

This multifunctional design adds privacy while creating multiple spaces for entertaining.

Sample Patio Plan 2

Sloping ground can be a challenge for patio plans, but can also be an opportunity for creating dramatic features or perspectives you can't get with a flat surface. In this backyard site, the area near the middle of the house was relatively close to grade. Adding a few retaining walls allowed the patio to extend out to both sides. One retaining wall cuts into the slope along the south end of the site, providing space and a boundary for a paver walkway linking the patio to the front yard. This abuts a four-foot-tall masonry wall that carves a 90-degree space into the slope and provides a backdrop (and backsplash) for an L-shaped outdoor kitchen.

The low wall at the north end of the patio retains earth for the patio surface and helps create a lofty feel for the sitting area outside the home's master bedroom. A planter with trees provides a subtle barrier between the sitting area and the main patio space. Out on the yard's planted slope, a set of stone steps leads to gently climbing stepping stone paths laid out for either strolling through the foliage or tending to garden plants.

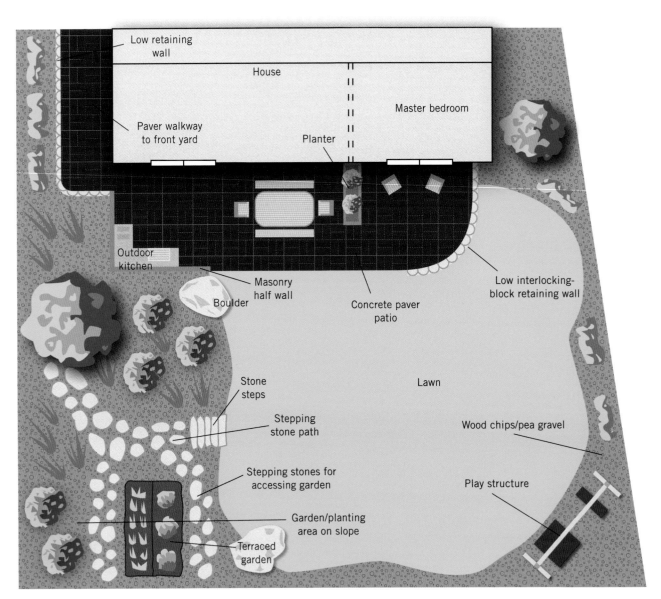

To make the most of a sloping yard, use retaining walls, steps, and paths to emphasize grand views and allow easy access to garden areas.

Sample Patio Plan 3

This grand design, created for a large suburban or rural property, has a setting for every mood and occasion: the expansive brick patio provides an elegant venue for both formal and casual entertaining. Guests (and kids) will feel more than welcome to step out onto the lawn for backyard games or a stroll through the grounds.

In addition to its ample open space, the brick patio serves as an entryway to a screened porch—a welcome retreat for hot, wet, or buggy weather. At the other end, the patio surrounds a small sun deck designed for a few lounge chairs or perhaps a bistro set used for drinks or everyday meals.

Away from the main patio, two destinations offer getaways of distinctly different character: follow the pebbled stepping-stone path through the archway to the sun-sheltered garden view from the gazebo. Or, stroll across the lawn after dark for stargazing around the open fire on the circular gravel patio.

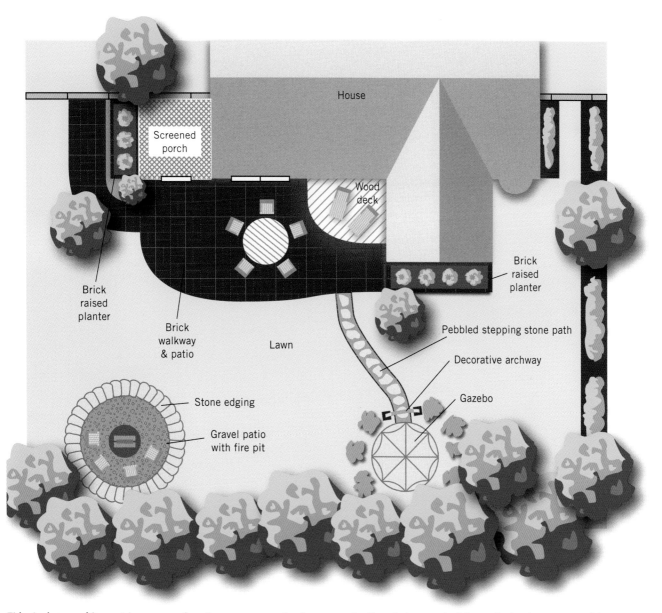

This design provides outdoor rooms for all purposes—gathering around a fire, dining, sunbathing, relaxing in a screened-in porch, or enjoying the view from a gazebo.

Sample Patio Plan 4

Casual and organic in feel, this plan with sandset flagstone surfaces embodies the spirit of the ranch home, in which the patio is used as an extension of the indoor spaces. Running the full length of the home, the patio is accessible from several different rooms and is likewise visible from each.

An arbor with vine-covered trellis screen defines and shelters a dining space located just outside of the home's kitchen. And for the cook, a large planting bed adjacent to the patio provides easy access to fresh herbs, fruits, and vegetables. An integrated sandbox keeps the kids near the house and out of the hot afternoon sun. Both the sandbox and integrated flowerbed are simply excavated areas filled with play sand over soil and landscape fabric.

In keeping with the natural look of the patio paving, flagstones are used for a well-traveled walkway between the front and back yards, while a compacted gravel path with natural stone edging creates an attractive service road leading from the shed to the back garden.

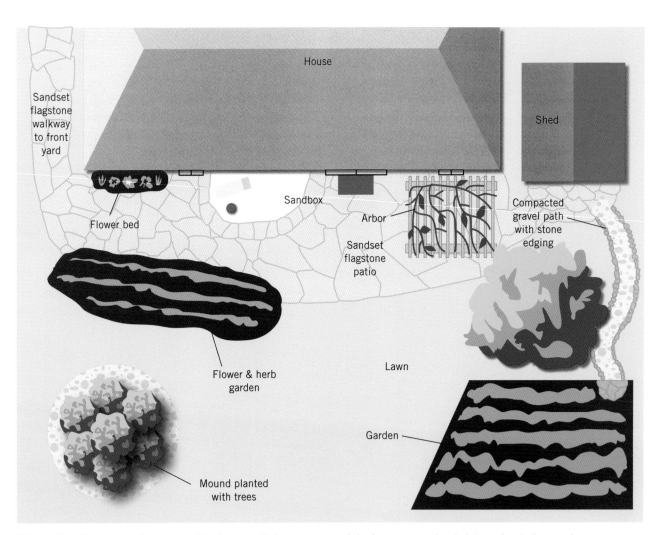

This sandset flagstone patio is accessible from multiple areas around the house, seamlessly integrating indoor and outdoor living.

Sample Patio Plan 5

This new suburban property presented a challenge to the standard patio plan: the back of the house seemed just right for a full-sized patio, but the neighboring property was so close that the view from the patio would be dominated by the neighbor's kitchen (and *their* backyard patio). The better view was from the front of the house. Therefore, this design places the main patio space around the front door, incorporating the existing entry stoop and portico. A second, smaller patio made with circular concrete pavers serves as a landing and casual sitting area just outside the door leading to the back yard.

Because it faces the street, is well-integrated with the house, and is partially sheltered with overheads, the entry patio feels a lot like a traditional front porch. A low masonry wall adds definition and a sense of enclosure to the patio. However, to maintain a welcoming feel for the front entry, a large opening in the wall leaves plenty of room for the existing concrete walkway. Also, the walkway remains uninterrupted from the sidewalk to the front stoop, clearly indicating the direct route to the front door. The patio paving is level with the walkway so the entire space is useable as a patio surface when needed.

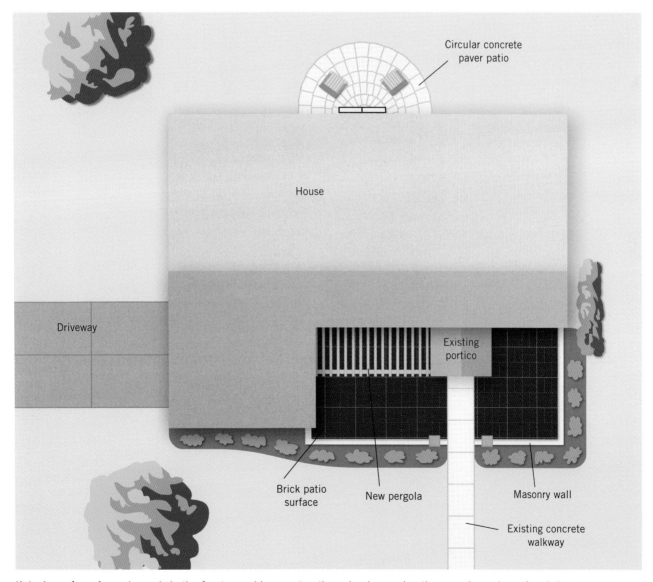

If the best view of your home is in the front, consider constructing a landscaped patio around your home's existing entryway, as shown in this design. A small patio in back is still a practical addition for greater privacy.

Patio Projects

A patio may appear to be a simple outdoor floor. But the functional factors that need to be considered, and the variables that any site poses, make laying a patio more complex than it might appear. Some decisions, however, will be made for you. Certain situations and soil types will preclude impermeable surfaces, for instance.

The projects in this section are intended to cover the gamut of potential patio surfaces. You'll find the range of options, from laying a concrete slab, to installing a sandset patio where efficient drainage is key. These projects also touch on how to beautify each type of surface, creating a patio that not only endures over time but looks good in the long run. So check out the installation possibilities and pick the one that makes the most sense for your design, your budget, and your yard.

In This Chapter:

- Layout + Surface Preparation
- Patio Edging
- Sandset Brick Patio
- Cobblestone Paver Patio
- Circular Paver Patio
- Mortared Paver Patio
- Sandset Flagstone Patio
- Mortared Flagstone Patio
- Concrete Slab Patio
- Tiled Concrete Slab
- Loose Materials Patio
- Loose-fill Patio with Firepit

Layout + Surface Preparation

The first major step of any patio project is to set up guide strings. Once that's finished, excavation begins and then a layer of gravel is added. The gravel is an essential element of patio construction: like your house's foundation, it creates a flat, stable base and it protects the surface material by providing drainage underneath to minimize shifting and settling caused by seasonal freeze-thaw cycles.

There are a few matters to take care of before you begin the layout and surface prep work. The first is to determine the thickness of each layer of the patio construction. This includes the thicknesses of the surface material, the sand bed (if required), and the gravel subbase.

For most patio types, the gravel layer should be 4 inches thick (after compaction). Concrete slab patios call for six inches of gravel, but this is subject to the local building code and may vary by region. The combined thicknesses of the layers minus the distance the patio surface will stand above the ground gives you the depth of the excavation.

The height of the finished patio aboveground is up to you. The standard minimum height is one inch. This ensures the patio will drain properly, but it's low enough to cut any bordering grass with a mower.

The next factor to determine is the total drop distance—the change in elevation from the high end to the low end of the patio surface. This creates the slope necessary for water runoff. Your patio should slope away from the house foundation or other adjacent structure (and preferably away from main traffic routes) at a rate of ⅛-inch per linear foot. For example, if your patio will extend 12 feet from your house, the drop distance of the patio surface will be 1½ inches. In the following project, you'll calculate the drop distance by measuring from the house (or high edge of the patio) to the batterboards at the low edge. The batterboards are set about 12" beyond the finished patio edges, and this additional amount makes the final drop distance more accurate than using the finished patio dimensions.

The final step before you start digging is to locate underground utility lines in the project site. Call your local utility to have your lines marked.

TOOLS + MATERIALS

Drill	Plumb bob
Circular saw	Scrap lumber (2 × 2, 2 × 4)
Hammer	
Level	2½" coarse-thread drywall screws
Hand maul	
Mason's string	Common nails
Line level	Compactable gravel
Power sod cutter or lawn edger	Eye protection
	Work gloves
Excavation tools	Rope or garden hose
Bow rake	Marking paint
Plate compactor or hand tamp	Flat spade
	U-shaped wire stakes (optional)
Shovel	Landscape fabric (optional)
Wheelbarrow	

Set up batterboards for the layout strings so you can easily remove and replace the strings without losing the slope and layout settings. A story pole—measured against temporary cross strings—makes it easy to check the depth of each layer as you work. Remember to call 811 so utility companies can mark utility lines in or near the project site before excavating.

How to Prepare + Excavate a Patio Site

Construct the batterboards from 2 × 4 lumber and 2½" screws: cut the batterboard legs 24" long, and then taper the ends to a point. Cut the cross-pieces at 24". Align and fasten the legs perpendicular to the ends of the cross-pieces. Use a nail or screw at the top center of each crosspiece.

2 × 2 stake

Roughly mark the patio corners with 2 × 2 stakes. Cut the 2 × 2 ends to a taper (the greater the angle, the easier it will be to drive into the ground). Tap the tapered end into the ground with a hand maul or sledgehammer.

Batterboard

Drive pairs of batterboards about 2 ft. behind the stakes, holding them plumb and level. The tops of the crosspieces should be about 12" above the ground. If the patio abuts the house, drive a single 2 × 4 stake at each corner so one face of the stake is even with the planned edge of the patio.

Tie a mason's string taut between an outer batterboard nail and one of the house-side (or high edge of the patio) stakes. Attach a line level (inset) to the string and adjust the stakes as needed until the string is perfectly level.

High side

Begin setting the slope on the first layout string: stand the pole next to the batterboard and mark the height of the level mason's string. Measure between the house (or high side) stake to the batterboard, then calculate the drop distance for the string—a common slope is ⅛" per linear foot.

(continued)

Using the story pole as a guide, drive the batterboard down until the string is even with the drop distance mark. Make sure the crosspiece remains level across the top so the string's height won't change if you move the string later.

Set up the remaining three string lines so they are even with the outer edges of the finished patio and are just touching the first string. First install the two strings parallel to the house, and use the line level to confirm they are level. The final string (parallel to the first string) will have the proper slope when it touches the intersecting strings.

Variation: Use a rope or a garden hose to lay out curved or freeform patio edges. Mark the outline onto the ground with marking paint. Once you complete the subbase, you can repeat the process to guide the installation. Note: Curving patios still need a string layout to guide the excavation and base prep.

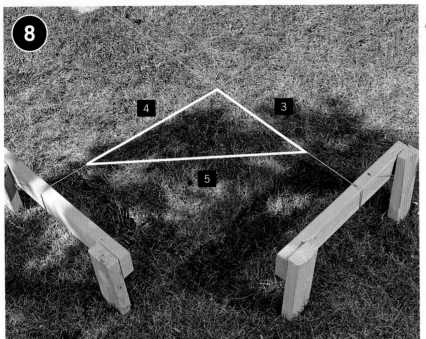

CHECKING FOR SQUARE

The traditional 3-4-5 technique can also be used for larger multiples of 3, 4, and 5. This provides greater accuracy for larger patios. For example, use 6, 8, and 10 ft.

Alternatively, you can use a long tape to measure between opposing corners of the layout. When the measurements are equal, the layout is square.

Make sure the string layout is perfectly square using the 3-4-5 squaring technique: starting at one of the string intersections, measure along one string and make a mark at 3 ft. (or a multiple of 3 ft.). Measure along the perpendicular string and mark at 4 ft. Measure between the two marks: the distance should equal 5 ft. If not, adjust the strings as needed until the measurements come out correctly. Repeat the process at the diagonally opposed corner. Mark the string positions onto the batterboard crosspieces.

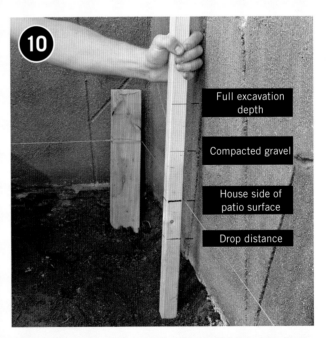

Determine the finished height of the patio surface. If the patio abuts the house, the finished surface should be 1 to 3" below the typical threshold of an entry door. At the low end of the patio it's desirable to have the finished surface rise at least 1" above the surrounding ground to facilitate drainage and prevent dirt and mud from washing onto the patio.

On your story pole, mark a top line for the distance from the string line (measured at the high edge of the patio) to the full excavation depth. A second line represents the distance from the string to the top of the compacted gravel base. Be sure to account for the thickness of the paving material and sand bed as needed.

(continued)

Cut the sod along the project outline using a flat-end spade or a power lawn edger. To compensate for edging, extend the excavation about 6" beyond the finished patio outline. Reserve healthy sod for covering soil backfill behind the edging.

Strip the sod or vegetation inside the outlined area and then excavate the construction area to a depth that allows for a 6"-thick gravel subbase, a 1" layer of sand, and the paver thickness; account for the finished height aboveground also.

Grade and compact the soil. First use a bow rake to achieve the proper slope, and then compact the soil with a rented plate or hand tamper. Set up temporary cross strings for reference to simplify the excavation and the gravel installation later.

Use the story pole to check the depth as you work. Drive a pair of 2 × 2 stakes outside of the original string layout, and tie on the cross string so it's just touching the layout strings. Check the depth at several points along the cross string, removing or adding soil as needed to achieve the proper depth. Once that's done, move the cross string to the next section and repeat. Note: Thoroughly tamp any soil that's been added to a low spot to minimize future settling. For the same reason, it's best to use soil from the immediate area (instead of purchased topsoil) or fill low areas with compacted sand or gravel.

Variation: For loose-fill patios, install a layer of high-quality landscape fabric to inhibit weed growth before adding the gravel base. Overlap rows of fabric by at least 6". If desired, pin the fabric in place with U-shaped wire stakes.

Add the first layer of compactable gravel. Dump heelbarrow loads of gravel into evenly distributed pods, then spread out each pod in all directions with a shovel and a bow rake. Use the rake to create a flat, smooth surface.

Thoroughly tamp each layer of gravel before adding more, as needed. If using a hand tamper, compact the gravel in 2"-thick layers; if using a plate compactor, compact every 4" of gravel. Use cross strings and the story pole to check the gravel height as you work. A straight 2 × 4 also helps for smoothing gravel prior to compacting and for checking for high and low spots.

Extend a plumb bob from the layout strings to the base to mark the exact corners and edges of the finished patio for the surface installation. Mark each point with paint or a small stake. Find and mark the corners of the patio by hanging the plumb bob from each string intersection. Proceed to the installation portion of your project.

Patio Edging

Edging can play many different roles in patio and walkway design. Its most practical purpose is containment—keeping the surface material in place so paving doesn't drift off into the yard. As a decorative feature, edging creates a visual border that adds a sense of order or closure to the path or patio space. This effect can be enhanced by edging with a material that contrasts with the surface material or can be made more subtle by using the same material, perhaps in a slightly different pattern. Finally, edging can serve to strengthen the patio or walkway as a hard, protective curb that stands up to years of foot traffic.

The best time to install edging depends on your application. For most sandset paving and loose material surfaces, edging is typically installed on top of the compacted gravel subbase. Edging along existing concrete slabs can be applied on top of the slab or along the sides, with the proper order determined by the finish materials.

To minimize the number of cuts required for paving, install edging after the patio surface is complete. You can also install two adjacent sides of edging to form a right angle, providing an accurate guide for starting the paver pattern, and then install the remaining two sides up against the laid pavers. A third option is to set up temporary 2 × 4 edging, which can be easily replaced with the real thing after the paving is finished.

Rigid Paver Edging

Choose heavy-duty edging that's strong enough to contain your surface materials. If your patio or walkway has curves, buy plenty of notched, or flexible, edging for the curves. Also, buy 12-inch-long galvanized spikes: one for every 12 inches of edging plus extra for curves.

TOOLS + MATERIALS

Maul

Snips or saw (for cutting edging)

Heavy-duty plastic edging

12" galvanized spikes

Install professional-grade paver edging along chalk lines (chalk lines are snapped directly below the outlines you've created with the mason's strings). The paver edge should rest on the compacted gravel.

Invisible edging is so named for its low-profile edge that stops about halfway up the side edges of pavers. The exposed portion of the edging is easily concealed under soil and sod or groundcover.

Rigid plastic edging installs easily and works well for both curved and straight walkways made from paving stones or brick pavers set in sand.

Brick pavers

Sand

Rigid plastic edging

Landscape fabric

Compactable gravel subbase

 How to Install Rigid Paver Edging

Set the edging base on top of a compacted gravel base covered with landscape fabric. Using your layout strings as guides, secure the edging base with spikes driven every 12" (or as recommended by the manufacturer). Along curves, spike the edging at every tab, or as recommended.

Cover the outside of the edging with soil and/or sod after the paving is complete. Tip: On two or more sides of the patio or path, you can spike the edging minimally, in case you have to make adjustments during the paving. Anchor the edging completely after the paving is done.

Brick Paver Edging

Brick edging can be laid in several different configurations (see below): on-end with its edge perpendicular to the paved surface ("soldiers"); on its long edges; or laid flat, either parallel or perpendicular to the paving. For mortared surfaces, brick can also be mortared to the edge of a concrete slab for a decorative finish.

TOOLS + MATERIALS

Flat shovel	Garden spade
Rubber mallet	Work gloves
2 × 4 (about 12" long)	Gravel
Bricks	Landscape fabric
Hand tamper	Eye protection

BRICK EDGING CONFIGURATIONS

Brick "soldier" edging with ends upward

Brick set on long edges

Brick set on faces, edge-to-edge or end-to-end

How to Install Brick Paver Edging

Excavate the edge of the patio or walkway site using a flat shovel to create a clean, vertical edge. The edge of the soil (and sod) will support the outsides of the bricks. For edging with bricks set on-end, dig a narrow trench along the perimeter of the site, setting the depth so the tops of the edging bricks will be flush with the paving surface (or just above the surface for loose materials).

Set the edging bricks into the trench after installing the gravel subbase and landscape fabric. If applicable, use your layout strings to keep the bricks in line and to check for the proper height. Backfill behind the bricks with soil and tamp well as you secure the bricks in place. Install the patio surface material. Tap the tops of the bricks with a rubber mallet and a short 2 × 4 to level them with one another (inset).

Stone Edging

Cut stone or dressed stone makes better edging than flagstone, which often has jagged edges that create an uneven border. Semidressed stone, with one or more flat sides, is a good option for a more natural look.

Trim irregular stones for a tight fit: first score a cutting line with a small stone chisel and maul, then complete the cut with a pitching chisel. Use a pointing chisel or the pick end of a mason's hammer to knock off small bumps and smooth rough edges.

Pitching chisel

TOOLS + MATERIALS

Rubber mallet	Sand
Maul	Eye protection
Stone chisel	Work gloves
Pitching chisel	Mason's hammer
Pointing chisel	Shovel
Garden spade	Gravel base
Edging stones	Landscape fabric

How to Install Stone Edging

Excavate the patio or walkway site and dig a perimeter trench to accommodate the stone edging. Add the landscape fabric and then a gravel base, as required. Place each stone into the trench and tap it with a rubber mallet to set it into the gravel. Use your layout strings to keep the edging in line and at the proper height.

Backfill behind the stones with soil and tamp with a shovel handle or a board to secure the stones in the trench. If desired, fill the spaces between stones with sand or soil to help lock them together.

Concrete Curb Edging

Poured concrete edging is perfect for curves and custom shapes, especially when you want a continuous border at a consistent height. Keeping the edging low to the ground (about 1 inch above grade) makes it work well as a mowing strip, in addition to a patio or walkway border. Use fiber-reinforced concrete mix, and cut control joints into the edging to help prevent cracking.

TOOLS + MATERIALS

Rope or garden hose
Excavation tools
Mason's string
Hand tamp
Maul
Circular saw
Drill
Concrete mixing tools
Margin trowel

Wood concrete float
Concrete edger
1 × 1 wood stakes
¼" hardboard
1" wood screws
Fiber-reinforced concrete
Acrylic concrete sealer
Eye protection
Work gloves

Concrete edging draws a sleek, smooth line between surfaces in your yard and is especially effective for curving paths and walkways.

How to Install Concrete Curb Edging

Lay out the contours of the edging using a rope or garden hose. For straight runs, use stakes and mason's string to mark the layout. Make the curb at least 5" wide.

Dig a trench between the layout lines 8" wide (or 3" wider than the finished curb width) at a depth that allows for a 4"-thick (minimum) curb at the desired height above grade. Compact the soil to form a flat, solid base.

Stake along the edges of the trench, using 1 × 1 × 12" wood stakes. Drive a stake every 18" along each side edge.

Build the form sides by fastening 4"-wide strips of ¼" hardboard to the insides of the stakes using 1" wood screws. Bend the strips to follow the desired contours.

Add spacers inside the form to maintain a consistent width. Cut the spacers from 1 × 1 to fit snugly inside the form. Set the spacers along the bottom edges of the form at 3-ft. intervals.

Fill the form with concrete mixed to a firm, workable consistency. Use a margin trowel to spread and consolidate the concrete.

Tool the concrete: once the bleed water disappears, smooth the surface with a wood float. Using a margin trowel, cut 1"-deep control joints across the width of the curb at 3-ft. intervals. Tool the side edges of the curb with an edger. Allow to cure. Seal the concrete, as directed, with an acrylic concrete sealer, and let it cure for 3 to 5 days before removing the form.

Landscape Timber Edging

Pressure-treated landscape or cedar timbers make attractive, durable edging that's easy to install. Square-edged timbers are best for geometric pavers like brick and cut stone, while loose materials and natural flagstone look best with rounded or squared timbers. Choose the size of timber depending on how bold you want the border to look.

TOOLS + MATERIALS

Excavation tools

Plate compactor (available for rent)

Maul

Reciprocating saw with wood-cutting and metal-cutting blades, circular saw, or handsaw

Drill and ½" bit

Compacted gravel

Landscape fabric

Sand (optional)

Landscape timbers (pressure-treated or rot-resistant species only)

½"-diameter (#4) rebar

Eye protection

Lumber or timber edging can be used with any patio surface material. Here, this lumber edging is not only decorative, it also holds all of the infill stone in place.

How to Install Timber Edging

During the site excavation, dig a perimeter trench for the timbers so they will install flush with the top of the patio or walkway surface (or just above the surface for loose material). Add the compacted gravel base, as required, including a 2 to 4" layer in the perimeter trench. Cut timbers to the desired length using a reciprocating saw with a long wood-cutting blade, a circular saw, or a handsaw.

Drill ½" holes through each timber, close to the ends and every 24" in between. Cut a length of ½"-diameter (#4) rebar at 24" for each hole using a reciprocating saw and metal-cutting blade. Set the timbers in the trench and make sure they lie flat. Use your layout strings as guides for leveling and setting the height of the timbers. Anchor the timbers with the rebar, driving the bar flush with the wood surface.

Lumber Edging

Dimension lumber makes for an inexpensive edging material and a less-massive alternative to landscape timbers; 2 × 4 or 2 × 6 lumber works well for most patios and walkways. Use only pressure-treated lumber rated for ground contact or all-heart redwood or cedar boards, to prevent rot. For the stakes, use pressure-treated lumber, since they will be buried anyway and appearance is not a concern.

TOOLS + MATERIALS

Excavation tools	Compacted gravel
Circular saw	Landscape fabric
Compactable gravel	Sand
Drill	2½" galvanized deck
2× lumber for edging	screws
2 × 4 lumber for stakes	Eye protection
Wood preservative	

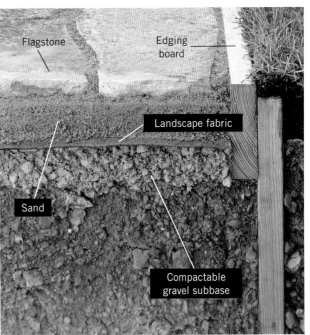

Wood edging is a popular choice for simple flagstone or paver walkways, and for patios with a casual look.

How to Install Lumber Edging

Excavate the patio site, and dig a perimeter trench for the boards so they will install flush with the top of the patio surface (or just above the surface for loose material). Add the gravel base, as required, including a 2 to 4" layer of gravel in the trench. Cut the edging boards to length, and seal the ends with wood preservative. Cut 2 × 4 stakes about 16" long. Set the edging boards in the trench and drive a stake close to the ends of each board and every 24" in between.

Fasten the boards to the stakes with pairs of 2½" deck screws. Where boards meet at corners and butt joints, fasten them together with screws. Use your layout strings as guides for leveling and setting the height of the edging. Backfill behind the edging to support the boards and hide the stakes.

Sandset Brick Patio

Traditional pavers set in sand make for one of the simplest yet most rewarding patio projects. The installation process is straightforward and, because there's no mortar involved, you can complete the work at your own pace. The overall installation time depends on the patio's design.

Square-edged patios require fewer cuts and thus less time than curved designs. But if you want something out of the ordinary, sandset brick or concrete pavers are great to work with—the small units are perfect for making curves and custom features; even if you have a lot of cuts, you can make them quickly and accurately with a rented masonry saw.

To pave with any of the classic patterns, such as running bond or herringbone, you'll start at one corner of your patio border or edging. To ensure accurate layout, check that the sides of the edging form a 90-degree angle at the starting corner. If you're not using edging or any kind of formal border, set up mason's strings to guide the brick placement.

If you go with clay brick without spacing lugs, use spacers cut from a sheet of ⅛-inch-thick hardboard to help set accurate sand-joint gaps as you lay the units.

Tape measure	Professional-grade landscape fabric
Circular saw	
Drill	U-shaped wire stakes (optional)
Excavation tools	
Mason's string	Rigid paver edging
Stakes	1"-dia. pipe
Line level	Coarse sand
Plate compactor (available for rent)	Straight 2 × 4
	⅛" hardboard
Hand tamp	Plywood scrap
4-ft. level	Paver joint sand
Rubber mallet	Rake
Push broom	Trowel
Brick paver units	Masonry saw
Lumber (2 × 2, 2 × 4)	Eye protection
	Maul
2½" drywall screws	Galvanized spikes (for edging)
Compactable gravel	
Work gloves	

Brick pavers set in sand create a classic patio surface that's more casual than mortared pavers. The inherent flexibility of the sandset finish allows for easy repair and maintenance or changes in the design over time. It also creates good drainage.

How to Install a Sandset Brick Patio

Set up batterboards and layout strings in a square or rectangle that's about 1 ft. larger than the excavation area (see pages 43 to 47 for detailed steps on layout and site preparation). Measure to make sure the string layout is square, and set the strings to follow a ⅛" per foot downward slope in the desired direction using a line level for guidance. Mark the excavation corners with stakes. The edges of the excavation should extend about 6" beyond the finished patio footprint.

Remove all sod and vegetation inside the area, reserving healthy sod for patching in around the finished patio.

Excavate the area to a depth that allows for a 6"-thick gravel subbase, a 1" layer of sand, and the paver thickness; account for the desired height of the finished surface above the surrounding ground. Use cross strings and a story pole to check the depth as you work.

Add an even 3"-layer of compactable gravel over the entire site, and then tamp with a plate compactor. Repeat with another 3" layer. The completed 6" gravel base prior to compacting must be smooth and flat, and it must follow the slope of the layout strings.

Install a layer of high-quality landscape fabric. Overlap rows of fabric by at least 6". If desired, pin the fabric in place with U-shaped wire stakes.

(continued)

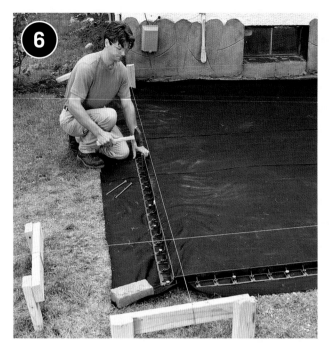

Install rigid paver edging along two adjacent sides of the patio area, creating a perfect 90° corner. Option: If you've laid out the pavers and taken precise measurements, you can install edging along three or four sides of the patio, as desired. Trim the fabric along the back of the edging. Lay down lengths of 1"-dia. pipe in parallel lines about 3 to 6 ft. apart.

Add a 1"-thick layer of coarse sand. Smooth it out with a rake so it just covers the pipes. Dampen the sand with water, then pack it down lightly with a hand tamp.

Screed the sand perfectly flat using a straight, long 2 × 4: rest the board on top of the pipes, and pull it backward with a side-to-side sawing motion. Fill in low spots with sand as you work. Dampen, tamp, and screed the sand again until the surface is smooth and flat and firmly packed. Remove the pipe(s) in the area where you will begin the paving.

Fill the depression left by the pipe with sand, and then smooth it out with a short board or a trowel. Tamp the area with the hand tamp, and smooth again as needed so the filled-in area is perfectly flat. Note: Repeat this step as needed during the paving process.

Begin setting the border bricks, starting at the right-angle corner of the patio edging, using ⅛" hardboard spacers if necessary. Complete the border row that will be parallel to the first course of field brick, and continue several feet up the perpendicular side edge. For gentle curves, use full bricks set with slightly angled (wedge-shaped) sand joints; tighter curves require cut bricks for a good fit.

Set the first course of field brick. These bricks should be centered over the sand joints of the completed border row. Use a mason's string tied between two bricks to align the leading edges of the first-course bricks. After setting several bricks, tap them with a rubber mallet to bed them into the sand layer. Complete the first field course, and then add some border units along the edge.

Field units

Border units

Snug a piece of edging against the installed brick and anchor it in place. Note: Install the remaining edging as the paving progresses. Continue setting the brick using the mason's string and spacers for consistent spacing and alignment.

CUTTING PAVERS + BRICKS

If your design requires cuts, use a masonry saw (tub saw). These water-lubricated cutting tools are available for rent at most building centers and stone yards.

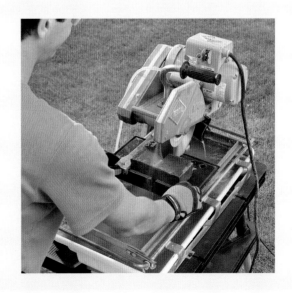

(continued)

Check each 4-ft. section for level to make sure the bricks are even across the top. Remove low or high bricks and add or remove sand beneath to bring them flush with the surrounding bricks. Work atop a plywood platform to prevent displacing the bricks. Complete the paving.

Variation: If your patio design includes curves or rounded corners, mark bricks for cutting curves by holding each brick in position and marking the desired cutting line onto the top face, then make the cuts with a masonry saw. For complex curves, it might be easier to leave off the border bricks and run the field brick long at the edges, then mark the curved cuts onto the field brick.

Spread sand over the surface, then sweep the sand to fill the joints. Sweep the surface clean, and then tamp the surface with the plate compactor to settle the sand in the joints and lock the bricks in place.

Fill and tamp the sand joints one or more times until the joints are completely filled after compaction. Sweep up any loose sand.

Soak the surface with water and let it dry. If necessary, fill and tamp again, then hose off the surface and let it dry.

90° herringbone patterns require bricks that are twice as long as they are wide. Start the pattern with two bricks set in the corner of your edging (edging must form a precise 90° angle). Add half-bricks next to the ends of the first two bricks. Complete the next row, zigzagging full bricks following the first row. Repeat the zigzag pattern for the remaining field bricks, adding half-bricks at the ends of rows as needed.

45° herringbone patterns require bricks that are twice as long as they are wide. Starting from a precise 90° corner, set the first row with two right-angle half-bricks. Complete the second row with two right-angle half-bricks flanking a full brick. Begin each remaining field row zig-zagging full bricks and finishing with right-angle half-bricks or trimmed bricks beveled at 45°.

Basketweave patterns require bricks that are twice as long as they are wide. To avoid cuts (on square or rectangular patios), you can install edging on only one side and use it as a baseline for the paving. Install the remaining three sides of edging after all bricks are laid. Snap a chalk line down the center of the sand bed, making sure it is perpendicular (90°) to the baseline edging. Working from the centerline out for each section, lay bricks in a pyramid shape, setting 12 bricks total in the first row, 8 in the second row, and 4 in the third row. Complete the paving by adding to each row incrementally to maintain the pyramid shape. This ensures that every row stems from the centerline to keep the layout straight.

Pinwheels allow you to avoid cuts (on square or rectangular patios) by installing edging on only two adjacent sides, starting from a precise 90° corner. Install the remaining edging after the paving is complete. Set each square pattern using four full bricks, as shown here, then fill the center cavity with a half-brick. For added accent, the centerpiece can be a unique color, but it must be the same thickness as the full bricks. Do not use a thinner brick for the center and compensate for the difference with additional sand; the brick will eventually sink and create an uneven surface.

These convenient interlocking pavers are made with DIYers in mind. They are easy to install and often come with fully plotted patterns for simple design preparation and installation.

Cobblestone Paver Patio

Concrete pavers have advanced by leaps and bounds from the monochromatic, cookie-cutter bricks and slabs associated with first-generation versions. The latest products feature subtle color blends that lend themselves well to organic, irregular patterns. A tumbling process during manufacturing can further "age" the pavers so they look more like natural cobblestones. The technological advances in the casting and finishing processes have become so sophisticated that a well-selected concrete paver patio could look as suitable in a traditional European square as in a suburban backyard.

When choosing pavers for a patio, pick a style and blend of shapes and sizes that complements your landscape. Match the materials used on your house's exterior and other stone or masonry in your yard to inform your decisions on colors and shade. Be aware that some paver styles require set purchase amounts, and it's not always possible to return partially used pallets of material, so order carefully.

In this project, we lay a cobblestone patio that uses three sizes of pavers. Such pavers may be purchased by a fraction of a pallet, or band, minimizing leftovers. We've also included a row of edge pavers to create a pleasing border around the patio. When shopping for your own patio materials, bring a drawing of your patio plans with exact measurements to your stone yard or landscape supplier. Based on your chosen pattern, the sales staff will be able to tell you how much stone in each size you'll need to purchase.

The patio in this project was created using the following sizes and proportions of cobblestone concrete pavers:

Field pavers—70 percent 6 × 9" cobble rectangles, 30 percent 6 × 6" cobble squares

Border pavers—3 × 6" cobble rectangles

TOOLS + MATERIALS

Excavation tools	Plate compactor
Wheelbarrow	Masonry saw
4-ft. level	Push broom
Hand maul	Concrete pavers
Wood stakes	Compactable gravel
Chalk line	Coarse sand
Mason's string	Plastic edging and spikes
Line level	Joint sand
Square-nose spade	Eye protection
1"-dia. metal pipes	Work gloves
2 × 4 lumber	Tape measure
Scrap plywood	Shovel

COBBLESTONES

Today, the word *cobblestone* more often refers to cast concrete masonry units that mimic the look of natural cobblestones. Although they are tumbled to give them a slightly aged appearance, cast concrete cobbles are more uniform in shape, size, and color. This is an advantage when it comes to installation, but purists object to the appearance.

COBBLESTONE PAVER PATIO—CONSTRUCTION DETAILS

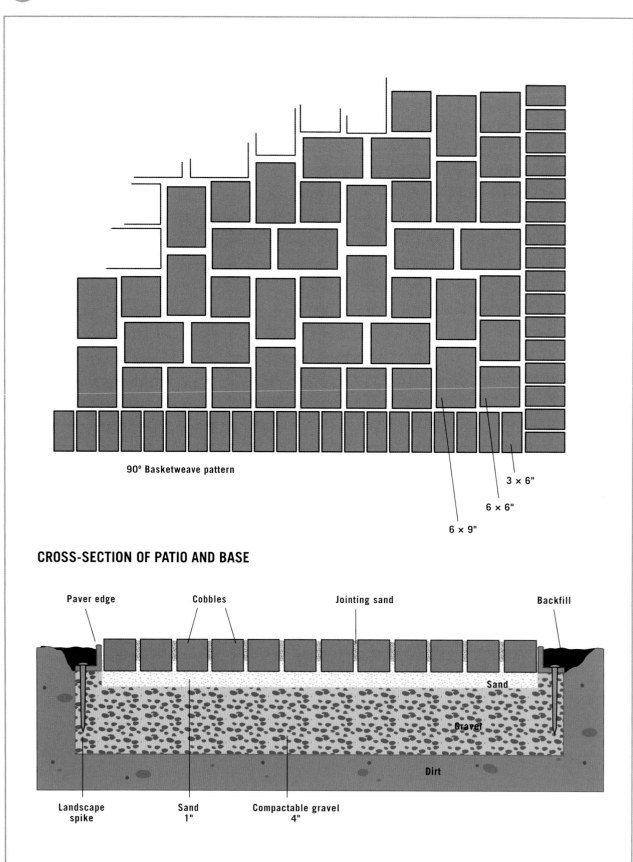

90° Basketweave pattern

3 × 6"

6 × 6"

6 × 9"

CROSS-SECTION OF PATIO AND BASE

Paver edge

Cobbles

Jointing sand

Backfill

Sand

Gravel

Dirt

Landscape
spike

Sand
1"

Compactable gravel
4"

How to Lay a Cobblestone Paver Patio

Mark the corners of the finished patio with stakes, and remove any sod or other plantings in the area. Set up grade stakes and mason's strings to guide the excavation and establish a downward slope of ⅛" per foot away from the house foundation.

Variation: Use batterboards and mason's strings to establish the layout of the project area. See pages 43 to 47 for detailed instructions.

Excavate the site to a depth that accommodates a 4" gravel subbase, a 1" layer of sand, and the thickness of the pavers (minus the desired height above the ground). Extend the excavation 6" beyond the patio footprint. Use the layout strings or grade stakes to check the depth and slope as you work. Tamp the soil with a plate compactor.

Add compactable gravel for a 4"-thick layer after compaction. Screed the gravel flat with a straight 2 × 4 and use a level or the layout strings to make sure the surface is properly sloped. Compact the gravel thoroughly with a plate compactor.

(continued)

Set up a new string layout to guide the edging installation using stakes and mason's string. The strings should represent the inside edges of the edging material. To make sure the layout has square corners, measure diagonally between the corners: the layout is square when the measurements are equal.

Install rigid paver edging along one side edge of the patio: snap a chalk line directly under the layout string along the edge, and then remove that string. Set the edging to the line and secure it with paver edge spikes, driving in the spikes only partially (in case you have to make adjustments later).

Rigid paver edge

Paver edge spikes

Screed (2 × 4)

Screed guides (1" pipe)

Lay lengths of 1"-dia. metal pipe in the project area to serve as screed guides. Fill the patio area with coarse building sand to the tops of the pipes. Screed the sand smooth and flat using a long, straight 2 × 4, pulling the board back and forth with a sawing motion. Remove the pipes, fill the voids with sand, and smooth the surface flat. *Tip: Dampen the sand before screeding.*

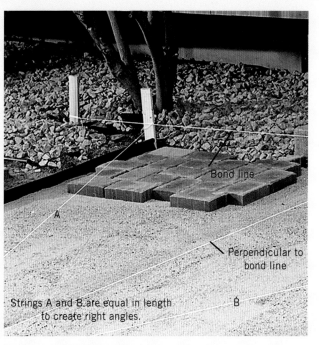

Set the pavers in the chosen pattern, starting at the 90° corner formed by the patio edging and an adjacent layout string (called the bond line). Lay border pavers along one or both edges before setting the field pavers. For now, simply lay the pavers in place; later, you will bed them into the sand with the plate vibrator.

Option: Use additional layout strings to help guide the paver pattern. Set up a string that is perpendicular to the bond line, using it to align courses every few feet. Tie equidistant strings between the corners and the end of the perpendicular string to assure a right angle with the bond line.

Install the remaining pieces of edging as you near the opposite side and end of the patio, leaving enough room for the final course of field pavers (plus border units, if applicable). Cut away the edges of the sand bed so the edging rests on the gravel base only. *Tip: If you don't need to cut pavers along the edges, you can install the edging after all of the pavers are laid.*

Cut pavers to fit as needed to complete the paving using a rented masonry saw (also see Making Curves on page 68). It's preferable to cut pavers a little too small than to have very tight fits; the joint sand will fill small gaps. With the paving complete, drive the edging stakes into the rigid edging to lock the pavers in place.

(continued)

Sweep joint sand over the pavers using a push broom. Continue adding sand and sweeping until the joints between pavers are nearly filled to the top surface.

MAKING CURVES

At rounded corners and curves, install border pavers (A) in a fan pattern with even gaps between the pavers. Gentle curves may accommodate full-sized border pavers, but for sharper turns you usually need to cut tapers into the paver edges so you don't end up with wide gaps at the outside. When using border pavers in a curved layout, the field pavers will need to be trimmed to fit the odd spaces created where the field and borders intersect (B).

Tamp the patio surface with the plate compactor. Move the compactor in circular motions, working from the outside in and overlapping rings as you go. Repeat Steps 10 and 11 until the joints are completely filled after compaction. *Note: Some paver manufacturers recommend sweeping excess sand from the pavers before compacting.*

CHOOSING PAVERS & PATTERNS

The number of options available when you shop for pavers makes it possible to create just about any patio layout pattern you can imagine. There is nothing stopping you from going wild and creating a layout that's truly one-of-a-kind. Most landscape centers will also work with you to create a layout for your patio that employs tested design ideas and uses pavers in a very efficient manner and with as little cutting as possible.

Another option for DIY designers is to visit the website of the paver manufacturer (you should be able to get the information from your paver dealer). Many of these have applications where you can choose a basic style you like (such as the patterns shown here) and enter the size of your planned patio. You'll receive a printout of what the pattern should look like, along with a shopping list for the materials you'll need, all the way down to sand and spikes for your paver edging.

A traditional brick running-bond pattern can be created using rectangular pavers.

This basketweave pattern is made with squares and large rectangles. A border of small rectangles completes the design.

Cobblestone paving with squares and large and small rectangles create this circular pattern.

Circular Paver Patio

Concrete pavers are available in a range of sizes and shapes, making it easy to create distinctive patterns without a lot of cuts. This circular patio is made with a complete set of shaped concrete pavers. To create a perfect circle, all you have to do is set the pavers following the manufacturer's installation diagram, and no cuts are needed (although some sets have center pieces that must be cut before installation).

Circular paver sets are commonly sold in fixed starter sizes, and you can add units as needed to enlarge the circle. You may have to purchase additional pavers as complete sets or in full-pallet quantities and use only what you need. Circular pavers are ideal for building freestanding patios because their shape makes for a nice decorative feature.

TOOLS + MATERIALS

Circular saw	Lumber (2 × 2, 2 × 4)
Hammer	Marking paint
Drill	2½" drywall screws
Excavation tools	Compactable gravel
Mason's string	Landscape fabric
Line level	1 or 1½" pipe
Plate compactor	Straight 2 × 4
Trowel	Washed concrete sand
Flathead screwdriver	Scrap plywood
Shovel	Plastic patio edging
Push broom	Paver joint sand
Circular paver units	Eye and ear protection
16d nails	Work gloves
Duct tape	Tape measure

A circular patio is visually dynamic and its shape makes it uniquely suited to intimate outdoor dining and entertaining spaces. When shopping for pavers, ask about color and texture options. Some suppliers may allow you to mix and match finishes for a personalized look.

As a design feature, a circle naturally draws the eye toward its center. This makes a circular patio the perfect setting for a round patio table and chairs or for highlighting a central decorative feature, such as a fountain or statuary. A circle is also the best configuration for creating an intimate seating area surrounding a fire pit. In addition to patio spaces, small circles can be used as landing areas along a curving paver walkway, while an open ring of circular pavers can be used as a border around a planting bed.

The patio in this project follows a standard sandset installation. Mortaring a patio like this would be far more difficult than sandsetting, due to the irregularity of the paver joints. For the sandset process, it's easiest to lay the pavers first, and then install flexible plastic edging around the perimeter to lock the units in place. If your patio plan calls for numerous cuts, rent a masonry saw, or *tub saw*, for making the cuts. Otherwise, you can make a few cuts with a circular saw fitted with a masonry blade. Before you get started, it will help to review the detailed information on laying out the project site and preparing the gravel base (see pages 118 to 119).

CIRCULAR PAVER MATERIALS

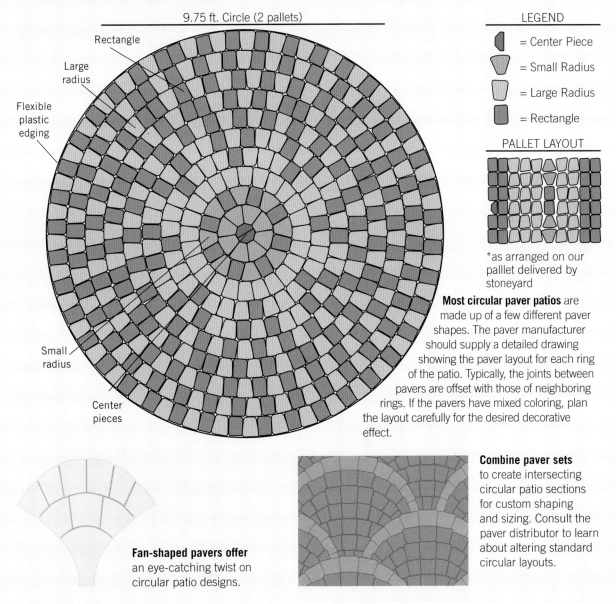

9.75 ft. Circle (2 pallets)

Rectangle
Large radius
Flexible plastic edging
Small radius
Center pieces

LEGEND

◗ = Center Piece
▽ = Small Radius
▱ = Large Radius
▯ = Rectangle

PALLET LAYOUT

*as arranged on our palllet delivered by stoneyard

Most circular paver patios are made up of a few different paver shapes. The paver manufacturer should supply a detailed drawing showing the paver layout for each ring of the patio. Typically, the joints between pavers are offset with those of neighboring rings. If the pavers have mixed coloring, plan the layout carefully for the desired decorative effect.

Fan-shaped pavers offer an eye-catching twist on circular patio designs.

Combine paver sets to create intersecting circular patio sections for custom shaping and sizing. Consult the paver distributor to learn about altering standard circular layouts.

Create a center pivot for defining the patio layout. Drive a stake at the exact center of the desired location for the finished patio. Cut a straight 2 × 2 about 12" longer than the radius of the patio. Drill a large pilot hole at one end of the board, and fasten the board to the center of the stake with a single nail. *Note: For large patio areas, use a string tied to a center nail instead of a board (inset).*

Mark the ground for excavation. Measuring out from the nail, mark the board at a distance equal to the radius, plus 6". Tape a can of marking paint to the board so the spray nozzle is centered on the mark (inset). Spray a continuous line onto the ground while pivoting the board to create a complete circle. Set up batterboards and leveled layout strings in a square that's about 1 ft. larger than the excavated area. Remove all sod and other vegetation inside the marked circle.

Measure diagonally to mark a traingle cutting equally across the circle. Adjust the strings as needed until the measurements are equal. Slope the layout strings ¼" per foot using the distance between the batterboards to calculate the drop distance generally dropping away from your house.

Excavate the site to the depth recommended by the paver manufacturer. Make sure the soil is smooth, well compacted, and properly sloped to ⅛" per foot.

Prepare the subbase with a 4" layer of gravel. Thoroughly compact the gravel with a plate compactor.

Check the depth with cross strings and a story pole as you work (shown). The completed base must be smooth and flat and follow the slope setting.

Install landscape fabric over the gravel subbase. Overlap the edges of fabric strips by 6". Trim the fabric as needed, leaving the ends a little long for now. *Note: This helps keep the sand base in place longer.*

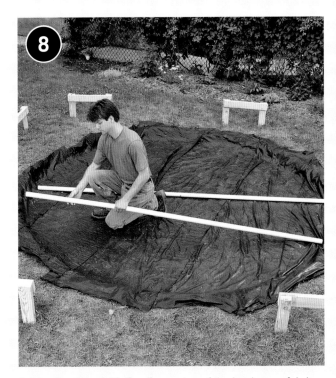

Set two lengths of 1"-dia. pipe on top of the landscape fabric so that one piece spans the full diameter of the gravel base and the other spans across the base about ¼ of the way in from the side of the circle. Align the pipes parallel to each other. Fill half of the patio site with sand even with the tops of the pipes.

Use a straight 2 × 4 to screed the sand level with the pipes. Move the short pipe to the opposite side of the site to complete the other half of the sand layer. Remove the pipes and then fill all depressions with sand. *Tip: Moisten sand prior to screeding.*

(continued)

Position the center paver, then measure out to the edge of the site in several places to confirm that it is centered. *Tip: Work on top of a piece of plywood to avoid disturbing the sand bed.*

Set the first ring of pavers around the center paver. Check their positions carefully, and make sure the spacing lugs are oriented correctly. If the pavers don't have lugs, gap them according to the manufacturer's specifications. *Note: Do not hammer or tamp the pavers into the sand bed unless the manufacturer directs otherwise.*

Set the remaining pavers, completing each ring according to your layout diagram. Be sure to offset the paver joints between rows. The pavers may be labeled, requiring them to be installed in a specific order as you work around the circle. After a sizable area is laid, work from your plywood platform set atop the pavers.

Install rigid paver edging along the patio's perimeter. Set the edging on top of the gravel subbase but not the sand bed. *Tip: Dampening the sand bed along the patio edge makes it easy to cut the sand away cleanly with a trowel before setting the edging.*

Inspect the paving to make sure all joints are aligned properly and all gaps are consistent. Make minor adjustments to pavers as needed using a flathead screwdriver as a pry bar. Be careful not to mar the paver edges as you pry.

Shovel joint sand over the entire patio surface, then use a push broom to sweep the sand over the pavers to fill the joints. Repeat as needed until the joints are completely filled, then sweep off excess sand.

Set the pavers into the sand bed using a plate compactor. Make a first pass along the perimeter of the patio, then compact the interior with parallel back-and-forth passes, overlapping the preceding pass slightly as you go. *Note: Avoid excessive tamping to prevent damage to the paver surfaces.* Add another application of sand. Tamp the surface, but make the interior passes perpendicular to those of the first tamping runs.

Refill the joints with sand a final time and sweep the surface clean. Spray thoroughly with water to settle the joint sand.

Mortared Paver Patio

Setting brick or concrete pavers into mortar is one of the most beautiful—and permanent—ways to dress up an old concrete slab patio. The paving style used most often for mortared pavers is the standard running bond pattern, also the easiest pattern to install.

Mortared pavers are appropriate for old concrete slabs that are flat, structurally sound, and relatively free of cracks. Minor surface flaws are generally acceptable, however existing slabs with significant cracks or any evidence of shifting or other structural problems will most likely pass on those same flaws to the final patio surface. When in doubt, have your slab assessed by a qualified mason or concrete contractor to learn about your options.

Pavers for mortaring include natural clay brick units in both standard thickness (2⅜ inch) and thinner versions (1½ inch) and concrete pavers in various shapes and sizes. Any type you choose should be square-edged, to simplify the application and finishing of the mortar joints. When shopping for pavers, discuss your project with an expert masonry supplier. Areas that experience harsh winters call for the hardiest pavers available, graded SW or SX for severe weather. Also make sure the mortar you use is compatible with the pavers to minimize the risk of cracking and other problems.

TOOLS + MATERIALS

Stiff brush or broom	⅜ or ½" plywood
Rented masonry saw	Spray bottle
Mason's trowel	Isolation board
Mortar mixing tools	Mortar
4-ft. level	Burlap
Rubber mallet	Plastic sheeting
Mortar bag	Notched board
Jointing tool	Mason's string
Pointing trowel	Straight 2 × 4
Concrete cleaner or pressure washer	Eye protection
	Push broom
Brick or concrete pavers	Work gloves

Nothing dresses up an old concrete patio like mortared pavers. The mortaring process takes more time and effort than many finishing techniques, but the look is timeless; and the surface is extremely durable.

How to Install a Mortared Paver Patio

Prepare the patio surface for mortar by thoroughly cleaning the concrete with a commercial concrete cleaner and/or a pressure washer. Make sure the surface is completely free of dirt, grease, oil, and waxy residue.

Isolation board

Mist the concrete with water to prevent premature drying of the mortar bed, and then mix a batch of mortar as directed by the manufacturer. *Tip: Install isolation board along the foundation wall if the paving abuts the house; this prevents the mortar from bonding with the foundation.*

Dry-lay the border pavers along the edge of the patio slab. Gap the pavers to simulate the mortar joints using spacers cut from plywood equal to the joint thickness (⅜ or ½" is typical). Adjust the pavers as needed to create a pleasing layout with the fewest cuts possible. Mark the paver locations on the slab and then set pavers aside.

Cut brick

Begin laying the border pavers by spreading a ½"-thick layer of mortar for three or four pavers along one edge of the patio using a mason's trowel. Lay the first few pavers, buttering the leading edge of each with enough mortar to create the desired joint thickness. Press or tap each paver in place to slightly compress the mortar bed. If necessary, cut bricks with a rented masonry saw.

(continued)

Remove excess mortar from the tops and sides of the pavers. Use a level to make sure the pavers are even across the tops, and check the mortar joints for uniform thickness. Tool the joints with a jointer as you go. Repeat the process to lay the remaining border pavers. Allow mortar to dry.

Option: To conceal the edges of a raised slab, build wood forms similar to concrete forms (see page 55). Set a gap between the forms and slab equal to the paver thickness plus ½".

Spacer

Notched screed

Dry lay the field pavers without buttering them. Use the plywood spacers to set the gaps for mortar joints. Cut end pavers as needed with a rented masonry saw. *Tip: Keep the courses straight by setting the pavers along a string line referenced from the border pavers.* Remove dry-laid pavers.

Spread and then screed mortar for the field pavers. Trowel on a ½"-thick layer of mortar inside the border, covering only about 3 or 4 sq. ft. to allow for working time before the mortar sets. Screed the mortar to a uniform ½" thickness using a notched board set atop the border pavers (set the interior end on a lumber spacer, as needed).

As you work, check the heights of the pavers with a level or a straight 2 × 4 to make sure all units are level with one another. If a paver is too high, press it down or tap it with a rubber mallet; if too low, lift it out and butter its back face with mortar and reset it. Repeat steps 6 through 8 to complete the paver installation, and then let the mortar bed dry.

Fill the paver joints with fresh mortar using a mortar bag to keep the paver faces clean. Within each working section, fill the long joints between courses first, and then do the short joints between the paver ends. Overfill the joints slightly.

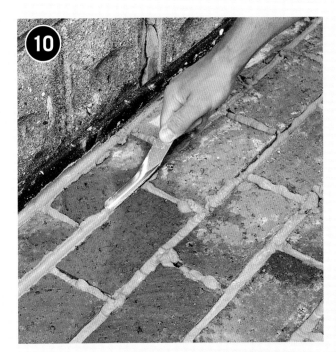

Tool the joints with a jointing tool—again, complete the long joints first and then fill the next section. As the mortar begins to set (turns from glossy wet to flat gray) in each tooled section, scrape off excess mortar with a pointing trowel, being careful not to smear mortar onto the pavers.

Let the mortar joints dry for a few hours, and then scrub the pavers with a wet burlap rag to remove excess mortar and any other residue. Cover the surface with plastic for 48 hours. Remove the plastic, and let the surface cure undisturbed for one week before using the patio.

Sandset flagstone patios blend nicely with natural landscapes. Although flagstone evokes a natural feel, the patio can appear rustic or formal. This patio has clean, well-tamped joints and straight, groomed edges along the perimeter that lends to a formal feel. Plantings in the joints or a rough, natural perimeter would give the same patio a more relaxed, rustic feel.

Sandset Flagstone Patio

Flagstones make a great, long-lasting patio surface with a naturally rough texture and a perfectly imperfect look and finish. Randomly shaped stones are especially suited to patios with curved borders, but they can also be cut to form straight lines. Your patio will appear more at home in your landscape if the flagstones you choose are of the same stone species as other stones in the area. For example, if your gravel paths and walls are made from a local buff limestone, look for the same material in limestone flags.

Flagstones usually come in large slabs, sold as flagstone, or in smaller pieces (typically 16" or smaller), sold as *steppers*. You can make a patio out of either. Larger stones will make a solid patio with a more even surface, but the bigger ones can require three strong people to position, and large stones are hard to cut and fit tightly. If your soil drains well and is stable, flagstones can be laid on nothing more than a layer of sand. However, if you have unstable clay soil that becomes soft when wet, start with a 4-inch-thick foundation of compactable gravel under your sand.

There are a few different options for filling the spaces between flagstones. One popular treatment is to plant them with low-growing perennials suited to crevice culture. For best results, use sand-based soil between flagstones when planting. Also, stick to very small plants that can withstand foot traffic. If you prefer not to have a planted patio, simply fill the joints with sand or fine gravel—just be sure to add landscape fabric under your sand base to discourage weed growth.

The following project includes steps for building a classic flagstone patio. If you're new to working with natural stone, see pages 86 to 87 for some basic cutting tips.

TOOLS + MATERIALS

Mason's string	Stiff-bristle brush
Line level	Circular saw with masonry blade
Rope or hose	Plugs or seeds for groundcover
Excavation tools	
Spud bar	Eye protection
Broom	Work gloves
Stakes	¾" plywood
Marking paint	3½" deck screws
1" (outside diameter) pipe	Pointing chisel
Coarse sand	Pitching chisel
Straight 2 × 4	Stone chisel
Flagstone	Hand maul
Spray bottle	Dust mask
Stone edging	Chalk or a crayon
Sand-based soil or joint sand	Square-nose spade
Lumber (2 × 2, 2 × 4)	Crushed stone
Drill	Ashlar
Mason's trowel	Mortar
	Capstones

ADDING A STONE WALL

A dry stone wall is a simple, beautiful addition to a flagstone patio. A wall functions as extra seating, a place to set plants, or extra countertop or tabletop space. It also provides visual definition to your outdoor space.

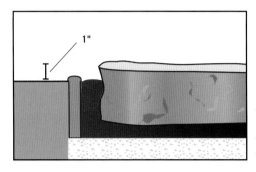

1"

Lay flagstones so their tops are approximately ½ to 1" above the surrounding ground. Because natural stones are not uniform in thickness, you will need to adjust sand or dirt beneath each flagstone, as needed.

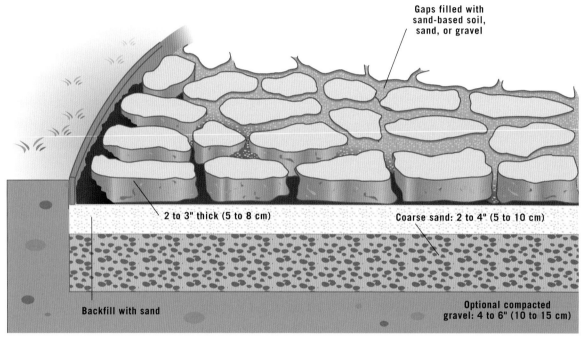

Gaps filled with sand-based soil, sand, or gravel

2 to 3" thick (5 to 8 cm)

Coarse sand: 2 to 4" (5 to 10 cm)

Backfill with sand

Optional compacted gravel: 4 to 6" (10 to 15 cm)

A typical sandset patio has a layer of coarse sand for embedding the flagstones. A subbase of compactable gravel is an option for improved stability and drainage. The joints between stones can be filled with sand, gravel, or soil and plants. Edging material is optional.

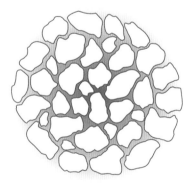

Irregular flagstones look natural and are easy to work with in round layouts.

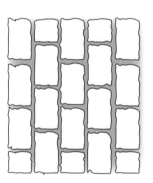

Flagstones that are cut into rectangular shapes can be laid in square or rectangular patterns with uniform gaps.

How to Lay a Sandset Flagstone Patio

Outline the patio base using string and stakes for straight lines and/or a rope or hose for curves. The base should extend at least 2 to 4" beyond the edges of the flagstones, except where the patio will butt up to a wall. Transfer the outline to the ground with marking paint. Remove any sod and vegetation within the base area.

Set up layout strings to guide the excavation using stakes or batterboards (see pages 43 to 47 for detailed steps on layout and site preparation). Excavate the base to a depth of 2" plus the stone thickness plus ½ to 1". Slope the ground away from the house foundation at a rate of ⅛" per foot.

Lay sections of 1" pipe across the project area to serve as screed gauges. These allow you to strike off sand at a consistent depth when you drag a screed board over them. *Note: Since large flagstones can be held in place adequately by the surrounding soil, edging for the patio is optional; it often looks best to allow neighboring groundcover to grow up to the edges of the stones. If you do plan to use edging, install it now.*

Fill the site with coarse sand slightly above the screed gauges. With a helper, drag a straight 2 × 4 across the screed gauges to level off the sand. Use a screed board that's long enough so that you can avoid stepping in the sand. Work the screed in a back-and-forth sawing motion. Remove the pipes once each section is finished, fill in the voids, and smooth the surface flat.

(continued)

Arrange your flagstones into groups according to size and shape. As a general rule, start paving with the broadest stones and fill in around them with increasingly smaller pieces, but appearance and sight lines are also important: if there is one nice stone with a flat surface and good color, feature it in the center of the patio. Or, if some of the patio will be visible from the house, choose nicer stones for these areas.

Begin by laying large, thick stones around the perimeter of the patio. Leave a consistent gap of about 1" between stones by matching pieces like a puzzle and cutting and dressing stones as needed (see page 87). The outer edge of the patio should form smooth curves (or straight lines) without jutting pieces or abrupt irregularities. Level stones as needed by prying up with a spud bar and adding or removing sand underneath.

Fill in around the larger stones with smaller pieces cut to fit the spaces, as needed, working from the outside in. After setting a band of stones a few courses wide, lay a 2 × 4 across the stones to make sure they're level with one another. Add or remove sand below to adjust their height, and dampen the sand occasionally to make it easier to work with.

Fill the joints between stones with sand-based, weed-seed-free soil. Sweep the soil across the patio surface to fill the cracks, and then water the soil so it settles. Repeat as needed until the soil reaches the desired level. Plant plugs or seeds for groundcover to grow up between the stones, if desired.

Variation: To finish the patio with sand instead of soil and plants, spread sand over the patio and sweep across the stones with a push broom to fill the joints. Pack the sand with your fingers or a piece of wood. Spray the entire area with water to help compact the sand. Let the patio dry. Repeat filling and spraying until the joints are full and the stones are securely locked in place.

 ## CHOOSING SOIL + PLANTS FOR YOUR PATIO

Sand-based soil (also called "patio planting" soil) is the best material to use for planting between flagstones. This mixture of soil and sand sweeps easily into joints, and it resists tight compaction to promote healthy plant growth, as well as surface drainage. Regular soil can become too compacted for effective planting and drainage and soil from your yard will undoubtedly contain weeds. Sand-based soil is available in bulk or by the bag and is often custom-mixed at most large garden centers.

As for the best plants to use, listed below are a few species that tend to do well in a patio application. Ask a local supplier what works best for your climate.

Patio "planting soil" (for planting between stones) is available in bulk or bags at most garden centers. It is good for filling cracks because the sand base makes it dry and smooth enough to sweep into cracks, yet the black compost will support plant growth. Because it is bagged, you can be assured it doesn't come with weeds.

- Alyssum
- Rock cress
- Thrift
- Miniature dianthus
- Candytuft
- Lobelia
- Forget-me-not
- Saxifrage
- Sedum
- Thymus
- Scotch moss
- Irish moss
- Woolly thyme
- Mock strawberry

You can cut most stone by placing it directly on a bed of flat, soft ground, such as grass or sand, that will absorb some of the shock when the maul strikes the chisel. If you plan to do a lot of cutting or splitting, construct a banker, a simple sand-bed table that provides a sturdy, shock-absorbent work surface (shown below).

For basic cuts and cleaning up stone faces (called dressing), the best tools are a pointing chisel, a pitching chisel, a basic stone chisel, and a hand maul. A circular saw also comes in handy for when you need a very straight edge or to help reduce the work of scoring many stones with a chisel. Always wear eye protection when cutting or dressing stone.

To build a banker for cutting stone, construct two square frames out of 2 × 2s, and sandwich a matching piece of ¾" plywood between the frames. Fasten the pieces together with 3½" deck screws driven through both sides. Fill one side of the banker with sand to complete the work surface.

Cutting Stone with a Circular Saw

A circular saw lets you precut stones with broad surfaces with greater control and accuracy than most people can achieve with a chisel. It's a noisy tool, so wear earplugs, along with a dust mask and safety goggles. Install a toothless masonry blade on your saw and start out with the blade set to cut ⅛" deep. (Make sure the blade is designed for the material you're cutting. Some masonry blades are designed for hard materials like concrete, marble, and granite. Others are for soft materials, like concrete block, brick, flagstone, and limestone.) Wet the stone before cutting to help control dust, then make three passes, setting the blade ⅛" deeper with each pass. Repeat the process on the other side. A thin piece of wood under the saw protects the saw foot from rough masonry surfaces. Remember: always use a GFCI outlet or extension cord when using power tools outdoors.

How to Cut Flagstone

Mark the stone for cutting on both sides using chalk or a crayon. If there is a fissure nearby, mark your line there, since the stone will likely break there naturally. *Note: To prevent unpredicted breaks when cutting off large pieces, plan to chip off small sections at a time.*

Score along the cut line on the backside of the stone (the side that won't be exposed) by moving a stone chisel along the line and striking it with moderate blows with a maul. As an alternative, you can do this step with a circular saw.

Break the stone to complete the cut: first, turn the stone over and rest it on a metal pipe or a 2 × 4 so the scored edge is directly over the support. Then, strike forcefully near the end of the waste portion to break the stone along the cut line.

Dressing Stones for Walls

Laying stones works best when the sides (including the top and bottom) are roughly square. If a side is sharply skewed, score and split it with a pitching chisel, and chip off smaller peaks with a pointing chisel or mason's hammer. Remember: a stone should sit flat on its bottom or top side without much rocking.

"Dress" a stone using a pointing chisel and maul to remove jagged edges or undesirable bumps. Position the chisel at a 30 to 45° angle at the base of the piece to be removed. Tap lightly all around the break line, then more forcefully, to chip off the piece. Position the chisel carefully before each blow with the maul.

Concrete Slab Patio

Few outdoor surfaces are as heavy-duty as a properly poured concrete slab. As a patio material, poured concrete is tough to beat. The surface is flat, smooth, easy to clean, and about as close to maintenance-free as you can get. A concrete slab is also the best foundation for permanent finishes like mortared brick, tile, and stone. And if you like the simplicity and durability of a bare concrete patio but flat gray doesn't suit your design scheme, you can always apply an acid stain, dry pigment colors, or concrete paint for custom coloring effects without compromising the surface's performance.

If you've never worked with poured concrete before, you'll find that most of the work lies in preparing the site and building the forms for containing and shaping the wet concrete. Once the concrete is mixed or delivered to your site, time is of the essence, and the best way to ensure quality results is to be prepared with strong forms, the right tools, and an understanding of each step of the process. And it never hurts to have help: you'll need at least two hardworking assistants for the placing and finishing stages.

This patio project follows the steps for building a small (100 square feet or so) slab that can be poured and finished all at once. The patio featured here is a circular, freestanding structure slightly more than 10 ft. in diameter. If the patio will abut your house, isolate it from the house with an isolation board and slope the surface so water drains away from the foundation. A smaller slab is much more manageable.

The moldable nature of poured concrete makes it ideal for creating patios with curves and custom shapes in addition to perfect squares and rectangles. If your patio plans call for an adjacent concrete walkway, see pages 148 to 153.

Larger slabs often require that you place and tool the wet concrete in workable sections, and these steps must continue simultaneously until the entire slab is filled and leveled before the concrete begins to set. It's a good idea to seek guidance from a concrete professional if your plans call for a large patio.

Because they are permanent structures, concrete patios are often governed by local building codes, and you might need a permit for your project—especially if the patio abuts a permanent structure. Before you get started, contact your city's building department to learn about permit requirements and general construction specifications in your area.

CONCRETE COVERAGE

VOLUME	SLAB THICKNESS	SURFACE AREA
1 CUBIC YARD	2"	160 SQUARE FEET
1 CUBIC YARD	3"	110 SQUARE FEET
1 CUBIC YARD	4"	80 SQUARE FEET
1 CUBIC YARD	5"	65 SQUARE FEET
1 CUBIC YARD	6"	55 SQUARE FEET
1 CUBIC YARD	8"	40 SQUARE FEET

Photo by **DIAKRIT**

A clear example of the dramatic surface that can be created in concrete once you've mastered pouring in forms, this bi-level structure includes a stunning matching firepit that seems to grow right out of the step-up area.

Drill	Plate compactor or hand tamper	Edger	2" wire bolsters
Circular saw		1" groover	Work gloves
Hand maul or sledgehammer	Eye protection	Magnesium trowel	Square-nose spade
	Plumb bob	Push broom	Isolation board and construction adhesive
Mason's string	Chalk line	Lumber (1 × 2, 2 × 4)	Concrete form release agent
Stakes	Hammer		
Marking paint	Hardboard lap siding	Compactable gravel	4,000 psi concrete (or as required by local code)
Line level	Bolt cutters	Screws	
Excavation tools	Concrete mixing tools	6 × 6" 10/10 welded wire mesh	Clear polyethylene sheeting
Bow rake	Shovel or masonry hoe		Lawn edger (available for rent)
Level	Wheelbarrow	Tie wire	
	Bull float		

Construction Details

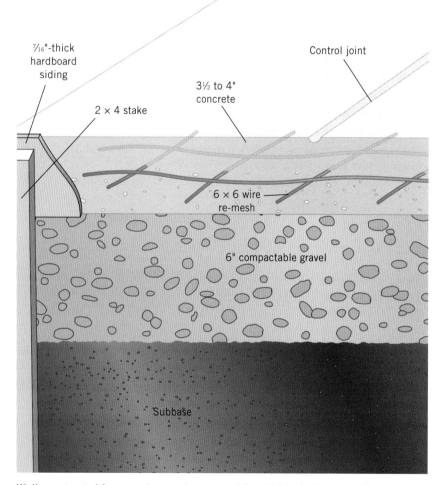

- ⁷⁄₁₆"-thick hardboard siding
- 2 × 4 stake
- 3½ to 4" concrete
- Control joint
- 6 × 6 wire re-mesh
- 6" compactable gravel
- Subbase

Well-constructed forms and properly-prepared foundational elements will ensure your slab is structurally sound.

WHEN IS CONCRETE READY TO FINISH?

Floating wet concrete causes the heavy materials in the mix to sink below the surface, leaving a layer of water—know as bleed water—on the surface. To achieve an attractive and durable finish, let the bleed water disappear before proceeding with the final finishing steps (edging, control joints, and finish troweling). How long this takes depends on the air temperature, humidity, and sun exposure; you just have to watch and wait.

Once the bleed water dries, test the concrete for hardness by stepping on it: if your foot sinks in no more than ¼", the concrete is ready for finishing. Be extra diligent with any areas exposed to the sun or wind, as they can dry much faster than other spots. *Note: Air-entrained concrete (commonly used for cold-weather pours) doesn't show bleed water, so you have to rely on the step test to know when it's time to start finishing.*

How to Build a Round Concrete Patio

Establish layout lines for the site excavation using batterboards, mason's string, and marking paint. Set the lines so they reach at least 12" beyond the work area on all sides. Plan for the gravel base to extend 12" beyond the slab. Use two pairs of perpendicular batterboards with strings to establish the centerpoint of a round patio (where the strings intersect). To create a rough outline for the patio excavation, drive a stake at the centerpoint and then attach a string to the top of the stake. Tape the other end of the string to an inverted can of marking paint so the distance from the stake to the can equals the radius of the circle, including the gravel base; mark the outline.

Cut the sod on the perimeter of the excavation area to define where to dig. For better access, first remove the batterboards (or at least the strings). A lawn edger works well for cutting the outline into the sod (be sure to wear safety equipment).

Story pole

Excavate the site for a 6 to 8"-thick compactable gravel subbase plus any sub-grade (below ground level) portion of the slab. If building next to your house, grade the soil so it slopes away from the house at ⅛" per foot. Measure down from the leveled cross strings with a story pole to gauge the depth as you work. Compact the soil after grading using a plate compactor or a hand tamper.

(continued)

If your patio will butt up to a house or another permanent structure, you should use the house or structure as your starting point for setting slope and establishing a patio layout. Snap a chalk line onto the house foundation at the precise elevation of the top of the finished slab. This should be 1 to 3" below any patio door threshold. You can use this line for reference during the site prep, the concrete pour, and finishing.

1 to 3"

Fill the excavation area with a 4"-thick layer of compactable gravel. Use an upside-down bow or garden rake to move the rock around. Rake the rock until it is level and follows the grade of the soil base.

Use a plate compactor to tamp the first 4" of graded compactable gravel. Add another 2 to 4" layer of gravel until the top surface will compact to the finished level. Use cross strings and the story pole to make sure the subbase is uniform and follows the ⅛" per ft. slope. Tamp until the gravel is compacted and at the correct height relative to your lines.

Set level lines for the form height. Replace batterboards and retie the mason's lines so they are level. If you are making a circular patio, as seen here, add intermediate stakes between the batterboards and the tie lines to divide the circle into at least eight segments. Drop a plumb bob from the point where the lines intersect, and drive a stake at this centerpoint. Use this stake to create a string guide and redraw the patio outline (inset).

Drive stakes for anchoring the forms around the perimeter of the patio, just outside the outline. Drive the stakes deep enough that they will be beneath the tops of the forms. Use a hand maul or sledgehammer to drive the stakes. To prevent them from splitting, use a scrap 2 × 4 as a hammer block to absorb the blows. Drive a stake at each point where a string intersects the patio outline.

Install forms. Here, ⁷/₁₆"-thick pieces of hardboard lap siding have been rip-cut into 3½" strips to make bendable forms. Cut each strip long enough to span three stakes as it follows the patio outline. Screw the strip to the middle stake first, making sure the top is the correct distance down from the layout string. Bend the form to follow the outline and attach it to the other stakes.

Drive stakes behind the forms anywhere where the strips require additional bending or anchoring to follow the round outline. Attach the forms to the stakes. *Note: If you are installing straight 2 × 4 forms, drive screws through the outsides of the stake and into the form boards to make them easier to remove later.*

(continued)

Lay wire mesh over the gravel base, keeping the edges 1 to 2" from the insides of the form. Overlap the mesh strips by 6" and tie them together with tie wire. Prop up the mesh on 2" wire bolsters placed every few feet and tied to the mesh with wire. If required, install isolation board along the house foundation.

Place 4000 psi concrete in the form, starting at the side furthest from the concrete source. Before pouring, construct access ramps so wheelbarrows can roll over the forms without damaging them, and coat the insides of the form with a release agent or vegetable oil to prevent the forms from sticking. Distribute the concrete with a shovel or masonry hoe. As you fill, hammer against the outsides of the forms to eliminate air pockets.

Screed the surface with a long, straight 2 × 4: have two people pull the board backward in a side-to-side sawing motion, with the board resting on top of the form. As you work, shovel in extra concrete to fill the low spots or remove concrete from high spots, and re-screed. The goal is to create a flat surface that's level with the top of the form.

Float the concrete surface with a bull float: without applying pressure, push and pull the float in straight, parallel passes, overlapping each pass slightly with the next. Slightly tip up the leading edge of the float to prevent gouging the surface. Stop floating once the surface is relatively smooth and has a wet sheen. Be careful not to overfloat, indicated by water pooling on the surface. Allow the bleed water to disappear.

Use an edger to shape all edges of the slab that contact the wood form. Carefully run the edger back and forth along the form to create a smooth, rounded corner. Slightly lift the leading edge of the tool as needed to prevent gouging.

Cut a control joint (if required) using a 1" groover guided by a straight 2 × 4. In most cases, you'll need to erect a temporary bridge to allow access for cutting in the center of the patio. Take great care here. Be sure to cut grooves while concrete is still workable. Make several light passes back and forth until the groove reaches full depth, lifting the leading edge of the tool to prevent gouging.

Flatten ridges and create a smooth surface with a magnesium trowel. This will create a smooth surface that takes a finish well once the concrete has dried. Another finishing option is simply to skip the additional floating. Then, before the concrete dries completely, brush lightly with a push broom to create a nonslip "broomed" surface.

Cure the concrete by misting the slab with water, then covering it with a single piece of polyethylene sheeting. Smooth out any air pockets (which can cause discoloration), and weight the sheeting along the edges. Mist the slab and reapply the plastic daily for 1 to 2 weeks.

Tiled Concrete Slab

Outdoor tile can be made of several different materials and is available in many colors and styles. Using natural stone tiles with different shapes and complementary colors, as demonstrated in this project, is a great way to draw attention to the elegant surface. Tile manufacturers may offer brochures giving you ideas for modular patterns that can be created from their tiles. Make sure the tiles you select are intended for outdoor use.

When laying a modular, geometric pattern with tiles of different sizes, it's crucial that you test the layout before you begin and that you place the first tiles very carefullly. The first tiles will dictate the placement of all other tiles in your layout.

You can pour a new concrete slab on which to install your tile patio (see pages 91 to 95), but another option is to finish an existing slab by veneering it with tile—the scenario shown here.

Outdoor tile must be installed on a clean, flat, and stable surface. An existing concrete slab surface must be free of flaking, wide cracks, and other major imperfections. A damaged slab can be repaired by applying a one- to two-inch-thick layer of new concrete over the old surface before laying tile.

TOOLS + MATERIALS

Tape measure	Paint roller
Pencil	Plastic sheeting
Chalk line	Thinset mortar
Tile cutter or wet saw	Modular tile
Tile nippers	Grout
Square-notched trowel	Grout additive
2 × 4 padded with carpet	Grout sealer
Hammer	Tile sealer
Grout float	Ear and eye protection
Grout sponge	Work gloves
Caulk gun	Mason's trowel
Tile spacers	Cloth
Buckets	Foam brush

Note: Wear eye protection when cutting tile, and handle cut tiles carefully—the cut edges of some materials may be very sharp.

Stone tiles can be laid as veneer over a concrete patio slab—a very easy way to create an elegant patio.

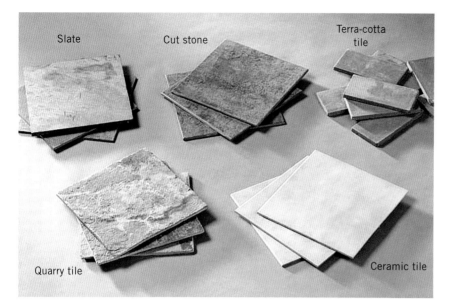

Tile options for landscape installations:
Slate and other smooth, natural stone materials are durable and blend well with any landscape, but are usually expensive. Quarry tile is less expensive, though only available in limited colors. Exterior-rated porcelain or ceramic tiles are moderately priced and available in a wide range of colors and textures, with many styles imitating the look of natural stone. Terra-cotta tile is made from molded clay for use in warm, dry climates only. Many of these materials require application of a sealer to increase durability and prevent staining and moisture penetration.

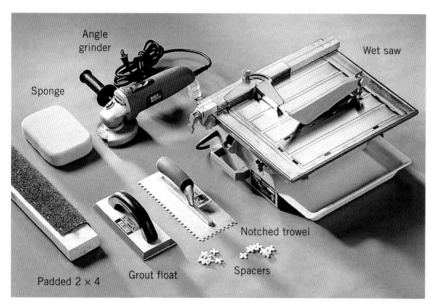

Exterior tile installation tools include:
a wet saw for cutting tile quickly and easily (available at rental centers—make certain to rent one that is big enough for the tile size you install), an angle grinder with a diamond-edged cutting blade (also a rental item) for cutting curves or other complex contours, a trowel with square notches (of the size required for your tile size) for spreading the mortar adhesive, spacers for accurate aligning of tiles and setting consistent joint widths, a straight length of 2 × 4 padded along one edge (carpet pad works well) for helping align tile surfaces, a grout float for spreading grout to fill the joints, and a sponge for cleaning excess grout from tile surfaces.

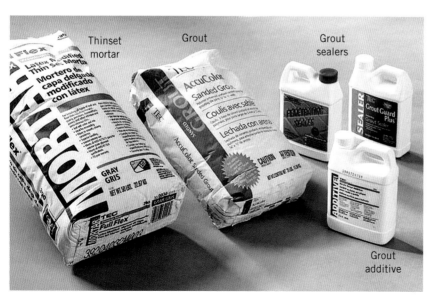

Exterior tile installation materials include: latex-modified thinset mortar adhesive that is mixed with water (if you can't find thinset that is latex modified, buy unmodified thinset and mix it with a latex additive for mortar following manufacturer's directions), exterior-rated grout available in a variety of colors to match the tile you use, grout additive to improve durability, grout sealer to help protect grout from moisture and staining, and tile sealer required for some tile materials (follow tile manufacturer's requirements).

Evaluating Concrete Surfaces

A good surface is free from any major cracks or badly flaking concrete (called spalling). You can apply patio tile directly over a concrete surface that is in good condition if it has control joints (see below).

A fair surface may exhibit minor cracking and spalling but has no major cracks or badly deteriorated spots. Install a new concrete subbase over a surface in fair condition before laying patio tile.

A poor surface contains deep or large cracks, broken, sunken, or heaved concrete, or extensive spalling. If you have this kind of surface, remove the concrete completely and replace it with a new concrete slab before you lay patio tile.

Cutting Control Joints in a Concrete Patio

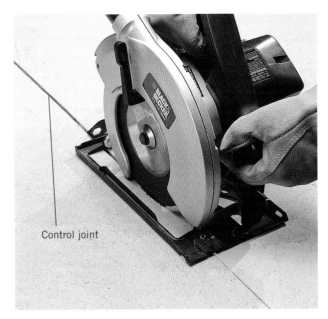

Control joint

Control joint location

Cut new control joints into existing concrete patios that are in good condition but do not have enough control joints. Control joints allow inevitable cracking to occur in locations that don't weaken the concrete or detract from its appearance. They should be cut every 5 or 6 ft. in a patio. Plan the control joints so they will be below tile joints once the tile layout is established (photo, above right). Use a circular saw with a masonry blade set to ⅜" depth to cut control joints. Cover the saw base with duct tape to prevent it from being scratched.

How to Tile a Patio Slab

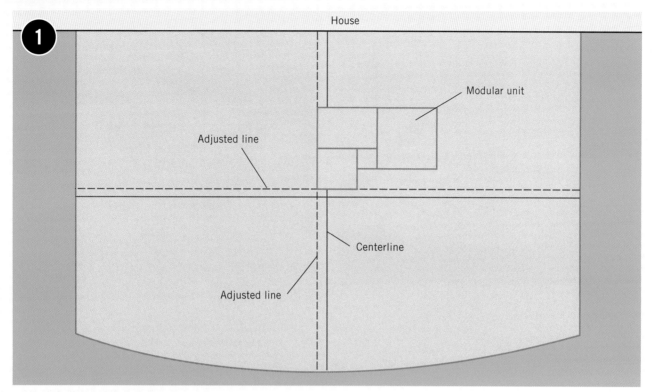

To establish a layout for tile with a modular pattern, you must carefully determine the location of the first tile. On the clean and dry concrete surface, measure and mark a centerline down the center of the slab. Test-fit tiles along the line—because of the modular pattern used here, the tiles are staggered. Mark the edge of a tile nearest the center of the pad, then create a second line perpendicular to the first and test-fit tiles along this line.

Make adjustments as needed so the modular pattern breaks evenly over the patio surface and is symmetrical from side to side. You may need to adjust the position of one or both lines. The intersection of the lines is where your tile installation will begin. Outline the position of each group of tiles on the slab.

(continued)

Variation: To establish a traditional grid pattern, test-fit rows of tiles so they run in each direction, intersecting at the center of the patio. Adjust the layout to minimize tile cutting at the sides and ends, then mark the final layout and snap chalk lines across the patio to create four quadrants. As you lay tile, work along the chalk lines and in one quadrant at a time.

Following manufacturer's instructions, mix enough thinset mortar to work for about 2 hours (start with 4 to 5" deep in a 5-gallon bucket). At the intersection of the two layout lines, use a notched-edge trowel to spread thinset mortar over an area large enough to accommodate the layout of the first modular group of tiles. Hold the trowel at a 45° angle to rake the mortar to a consistent depth.

Set the first tile, twisting it slightly as you push it into the mortar. Align it with both adjusted layout lines, then place a padded 2 × 4 over the center of the tile and give it a light rap with a hammer to set the tile.

Position the second tile adjacent to the first with a slight gap between them. Place spacers on end in the joint near each corner and push the second tile against the spacers. Make certain the first tile remains aligned with the layout lines. Set the padded 2 × 4 across both tiles and tap to set. Use a damp cloth to remove any mortar that squeezes out of the joint or gets on tile surfaces. Joints must be at least ⅛"-deep to hold grout.

Lay the remaining tiles of the first modular unit using spacers. Using the trowel, scrape the excess mortar from the concrete slab in areas you will not yet be working on to prevent it from hardening and interfering with the installation.

With the first modular unit set, continue laying tile following the pattern established. You can use the chalk lines for general reference, but they will not be necessary as layout lines. To prevent squeeze-out between tiles, scrape a heavy accumulation of mortar ½" away from the edge of a set tile before setting the adjacent tile.

 ## CUTTING CURVES IN TILE

To make convex (left) or concave (right) curves, mark the profile of the curve on the tile, then use a wet saw to make parallel straight cuts, each time cutting as close to the marked line as possible. Use a tile nippers to break off small portions of tabs, gradually working down to the curve profile. Finally, use an angle grinder to smooth off the sharp edges of the tabs. Make sure to wear a particle mask when using the tile saw and wear sturdy gloves when using the nippers.

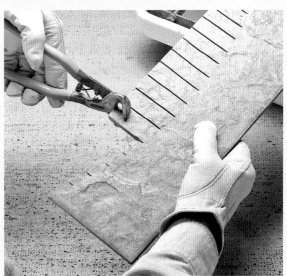

(continued)

After installing the tile, cover the tiled area with plastic, and let the thinset mortar cure according to the manufacturer's instructions. When tile has fully set, remove the plastic and mix grout, using a grout additive instead of water. Grout additive is especially important in outdoor applications, because it creates joints that are more resilient in changing temperatures.

Use a grout float to spread grout over an area that is roughly 10 sq. ft. Push down with the face of the float to force grout into the joints, then hold the float edge at a 45° angle to the tile surface and scrape off the excess grout.

Once you've grouted this area, wipe off the grout residue using a damp sponge. Wipe with a light, circular motion—you want to clean tile surfaces without pulling grout out of the joints. Don't try to get the tile perfectly clean the first time. Wipe the area several times, rinsing out the sponge frequently.

Once the grout has begun to set (usually about 1 hour, depending on temperature and humidity), clean the tile surfaces again. You want to thoroughly clean grout residue from tile surfaces because it is difficult to remove once it has hardened. Buff off a light film left after final cleaning with a cloth.

GROUTING POROUS TILES

Some tiles, such as slate, have highly porous surfaces that can be badly stained by grout. For these tiles, apply grout by filling an empty caulk tube (available at tile stores and some building centers) with grout, and apply the grout to the joints with a caulk gun. Cut the tip to make an opening just large enough to allow grout to be forced out. Run the tip down the joint between tiles as you squeeze out the grout. Remove the grout that gets on the tile surface with a wet sponge. You may need to use your finger to force grout into the joint—protect your skin by wearing a heavy glove to do this.

Cover the pad with plastic and let the grout cure according to manufacturer's instructions. Once the grout has cured, use a foam brush to apply grout sealer to only the grout, wiping any spillover off of tile surfaces.

Apply tile sealer to the entire surface using a paint roller. Cover the patio with plastic and allow the sealer to dry completely before exposing the patio to weather or traffic.

Loose Materials Patio

Gravel, crushed stone, wood chips, and other loose materials are very easy to install and are a surprisingly attractive patio surface. The versatile nature of loose material lends itself to everything from creative mixed-media designs to plain surfaces that evoke the simple beauty of Zen rock gardens.

The basic installation of a loose materials patio starts with excavating the site, then adding a two-inch layer of compacted gravel and edging material. Edging is required for this project to contain the loose surface material. From this point, the installation depends on the type of material you're using.

For crushed stone, gravel, and other small aggregates, add one to two inches of surface material and tamp flat; for river rock, add two inches or more (based on rock size); for wood chips, add at least a two-inch-thick layer and rake smooth.

For the smoothest, hardest surface, use a highly compactable material, such as decomposed granite (DG), for the finish material—or you can cover a coarser gravel base with granite fines (rock dust). Compact either surface with a plate compactor.

TOOLS + MATERIALS

Drill	2½" drywall screws
Circular saw	Professional-grade landscape fabric
Sledgehammer	
Mason's string	Compactable gravel
Line level	Edging
Excavation tools	Gravel or other fill material
Bow rake	
Plate compactor	Eye protection
Plumb bob	Work gloves
Lumber (2 × 2, 2 × 4)	

A loose material patio provides a casual, natural environment for any type of yard or garden. The surface is not as solid underfoot, so it is best used where that is not a concern.

How to Create a Loose Material Patio

Plan and excavate the site. Lay out the patio site with batterboards and mason's strings, planning for a slope of ⅛" per foot (see pages 42 to 47 for detailed steps on layout and site preparation). Excavate the site to a depth of 4" (or as desired, depending on the surface material and your application), and tamp the soil with a plate compactor. Cover the site with landscape fabric, overlapping the edges by at least 6".

Add compactable gravel and edging: cover the site with compactable gravel, rake it flat and smooth, and then tamp it thoroughly with a plate compactor. The layer should be about 2" thick after compaction. Install patio edging as desired, setting it at least ½" higher than the top of the finished patio surface to help contain the surface material.

Option: Install accent pavers. Set pavers (stone, concrete, wood, or other material) onto the gravel base, as desired. For flagstone and other materials that might not be flat on the bottom, add sand underneath to prevent wobbling.

Spread out the surface material over the patio area, raking it into an even layer of the desired thickness.

Tamp the surface material, if appropriate, with a hand tamp, plate compactor, or drum roller to create an even, flat surface. If the surface material is stone or other masonry, spray the patio with water to wash away dirt and dust.

Loose-fill Patio with Fire Pit

A fire pit makes a wonderful focal point for backyard gatherings. Many local codes stipulate that a fire pit area should be at least 20 feet across, including the surrounding circular area that can be outfitted with chairs and benches. Dressed with rock (trap rock is shown here), this area creates a safety zone between the pit and structures or combustible yard elements, such as landscape plants and dry lawns. For comfort and safety, fire pits should be installed only on level ground.

The fire pit featured here is constructed around a metal liner that you can buy from landscape supply centers. A liner will keep the fire pit wall from overheating and cracking if cooled suddenly by rain or a bucket of water. The liner seen here is a section of 36-inch-diameter corrugated culvert pipe. Other types of suitable liners are often sold as "barbecue rings" or "fire rings." Typically made of steel or iron, rings may include integral grills or have flanges for setting in a removable barbecue grate. The wall of the fire pit in this project is built with ashlar stones that are relatively uniform in size and have flat sides that make for easy stacking. But you can use any type of stone you like, as well as cast concrete retaining wall blocks. Whatever material you choose, set the wall stones on a solid foundation of compactable gravel, as with a paver patio. It's most efficient to prep the base for the seating area at the same time as the fire pit.

Note: We've shown the pit uncovered in all the photos here for detail clarity, but most local fire codes call for screens over fire pits. Screens of different sizes are available from large home centers and are a simple way to limit any fire risk.

TOOLS + MATERIALS

Wheelbarrow	Metal fire pit liner
Marking paint	Compactable gravel
Excavation tools	Dressing rock
Hand tamp	Wall stones
Plate compactor	Rake
Level	Eye and ear protection
Straight 2 × 4	Work gloves
Hand maul or sledgehammer	Stakes
1"-dia. pipe	Square-nose spade
Landscape edging	Fire pit screen

A loose-fill patio and stone fire pit is what you'd expect to find in the Old West or on trails deep in the forest. Why not bring this to your backyard? It's a simple DIY project that incorporates a compactable gravel foundation topped with a decorative rock or loose stone material and an excavated area reserved for the fire pit.

Construction Details

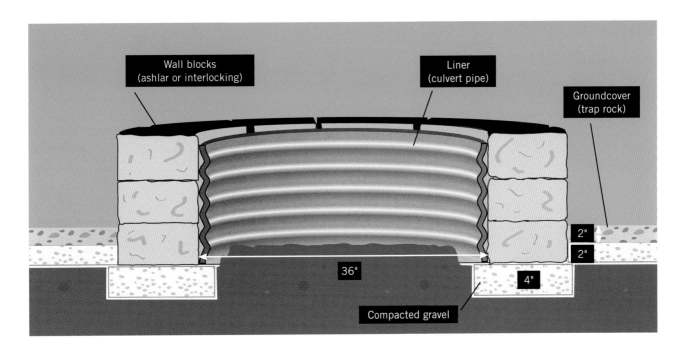

Wall blocks (ashlar or interlocking)

Liner (culvert pipe)

Groundcover (trap rock)

2"

2"

36"

4"

Compacted gravel

How to Install Rigid Paver Edging

1

Mark the patio outline: drive a length of pipe into the center of the pit area. Measure out from the pipe a distance equal to the outside radius of the seating area. Use a cord with a loop in it and a can of marking paint to draw a circle with this radius onto the ground around the pipe.

2

Cut out the sod and excavate the site to a level plane 4" below grade (or as appropriate for the surface material) over the entire circled area, from pipe to perimeter (leave the pipe in place for now).

(continued)

Excavate the fire pit wall area. Draw two more circles around the center pipe: an inner circle with a radius 6" smaller than the radius of the pit liner and an outer circle with a radius 6" larger than the outside radius of the finished fire pit. These lines mark the base for supporting the wall stones. Excavate an additional 4" down within this ring and compact the soil at the bottom of the trench with a hand tamp.

Fill the trench with compactable gravel and tamp it thoroughly so it is very hard. Fill the entire patio area with compactable gravel to 2" below grade. Use a level on a straight 2 × 4 to flatten and level the gravel (the area in the wall trench must be perfectly flat and level. Do not compact the top layer of gravel.

Position the metal fire pit liner so it is centered around the pipe and is perfectly level. Add or remove gravel beneath to level the liner, as needed.

Lay the first course of wall stones around the liner. Adjust the stones so they maintain a consistent spacing to the liner and between one another. Check with a level as you work to make sure the stones are level across the top.

Lay the remaining courses of wall stones, staggering the vertical joints between courses. If desired, top the fire pit wall with a cap row of smooth, flat stones. The top of the wall should be at least slightly higher than the edge of the liner.

Compact the gravel in the surrounding area with a plate compactor. This will stabilize the area and form a hard subbase that inhibits weed growth. Install the edging of your choice along the perimeter of the loose fill area.

Add a 2"-layer of top-dressing rock in the seating area, raking it flat and level. Compact the layer with a plate compactor. *Tip: Angular rock, such as the trap rock seen here, makes a better walking surface than smooth, rounded gravel.*

Nature-Friendly Patios

There are actually two types of "nature-friendly" patios. The first and most obvious is the outdoor surface that makes a minimal (or no) impact on the environment. The other type seamlessly blends into the home's outdoor surroundings, thanks to enlightened design and skillful installation. This section covers both types.

Patio material suppliers have made great progress in creating environmentally responsible paver and infill alternatives. These include recycled rubber chips and composite pavers made largely from wood waste and/or recycled plastic. Those are all easy to use and fit well in the right patio design.

But even if you're set on using more traditional materials, you can use them in thoughtful ways to ensure your patio blends with its natural surroundings. This is an excellent way to create a showcase patio that doesn't break the bank, but creates a totally unique visual. Patios designed with the natural environment in mind also ease the transition from indoors to out.

In This Chapter:

- Gallery of Nature-friendly Patios
- Creating a Permeable Subbase
- Spaced Masonry Pavers
- Composite Permeable Pavers
- Rubber Tile Patio
- Recycled Plastic Pavers
- Recycled Rubber Chips
- Subsurface Grids

Gallery of Nature-friendly Patios

Conventional pavers are nearly as good as permeable pavers when spaced apart. The gaps can be filled with grass, creeping plants, sand, or stone.

Grass or low-maintenance ornamental plants combined with conventional pavers look great, drain well, and return a little oxygen to the environment. Some, like Creeping Thyme, even smell good when you walk on them.

Simple concrete squares on a bed of gravel minimizes the environmental impact of this patio, and increases its visual allure. The theme is reinforced by classic wood Adirondack chairs, a metal fire pit, and a wood fence as a backdrop.

A minimal dining patio is tucked into the corner of a lushly landscaped backyard. Gravel between the pavers allows water percolation to ensure moisture makes it to the abundant plant life, and the patio seems a perfectly natural part of the landscape.

By adding drainage strips to your paver layout, you provide water with a place to flow back into the ground.

Permeable steps limit the erosion of surrounding surfaces as well as runoff. Here, chips of recycled rubber are bonded together and used as fill to create the step treads.

This brick patio surface set in a basketweave pattern is actually achieved with interlocking pavers made from recycled materials.

Creating a Permeable Subbase

Most patios made with rock or masonry units should have a stable subbase of compacted rock or gravel, usually beneath a layer of coarse sand into which the surfacing materials are set. Typically, these subbase layers are 6 to 8 inches thick, depending on your soil conditions—loose, loamy, or sandy soil needs a thicker subbase. A standard subbase made from compactable gravel (called Class II or Class V in most areas) hardens to form a solid mass when it is compacted. Water runoff will not penetrate such a subbase. But as patio builders have begun to place a higher value on water retention and minimizing runoff, they have developed permeable subbases that accomplish the same result by stabilizing the patio, but allow water runoff to seep through into the subsoil below instead of running off and into the wastewater collection system.

They key to a permeable subbase is called open-grade drainage rock in most areas. Where Class II and Class V are sifted with fine pulverized material (usually limestone) that hardens, ungraded drainage rock is just the rock. Most landscape materials stores carry it in two sizes: ¾ inch aggregate and 1½ inch aggregate. The prevailing wisdom suggests laying a layer of the larger rock first, compacting it, and then topping it off with a compacted layer of the smaller drainage rock before you put down your sand bed (if you are using one). Once you've created a permeable subbase, it will look very much like a traditional subbase and you build upon it using the same techniques.

However, note that a permeable subbase is of little value if you top it with an impermeable or minimally permeable surfacing, such as interlocking pavers. Use either material that allows water to drain through it (such as pervious pavers), or install impermeable materials with large enough gaps between the individual members that the water will run off the pavers or stones and drain down through the gaps.

A permeable subbase looks a little like a typical compacted gravel subbase, but because the open-grade drainage rock is devoid of fines it does not form a solid layer and thus it allows water to run through, not off.

Stakes and mason's line

Tape measure

Maul

Shovels or other excavation tools

Wheelbarrow

Hand tamper

Landscape rake

Plate compactor

Level

Ear and eye protection

Sturdy shoes/boots

Work gloves

Large (1½" diameter) open-grade drainage rock

Smaller (¾" diameter) open-grade rock

Landscape fabric or geogrid textile (optional)

Edging

Coarse sand or pulverized granite (optional)

Coarse setting sand

¾"-dia. open-grade drainage rock

1½"-dia. open-grade drainage rock

The thickness of your permeable subbase depends on the soil conditions. For stable soil with good drainage, a 4 to 6" subbase is adequate. If you have loamy or sandy soil, go as thick as 10", with a layer of larger-diameter drainage rock. Adding an underlayment of geogrid textile will help stabilize the subbase in such cases. An underlayment is not helpful in stable soil with good drainage.

Pavers

Coarse setting sand

¾"-dia. open-grade drainage rock (2 to 4 inches)

1½"-dia. open-grade limestone (4 to 6 inches)

Geotextile

The components of a permeable subbase, from bottom to top, include a 4 to 6" layer of 1½" diameter open-grade drainage rock (limestone is shown here); above that, a 2 to 4" layer of open-grade rock; a top layer of coarse sand or pulverized granite for use as a setting bed for flagstone or masonry units.

How to Install a Permeable Subbase

Drive corner posts and outline the patio area. Run mason's lines between the corner posts. Ideally, the patio should slope away from an adjoining house at a rate of around ½" for every 10 ft. Set a level line along the edges of the patio perpendicular to the house. Adjust the line downward to create the slope.

Begin excavating the site. A typical permeable subbase is 8" below grade when you allow for the thickness of the setting layer and the pavers or other surfacing. Use your layout strings to establish your digging depth. Measure the distance from the mason's line to the ground and add the depth of your excavation—8" in the project seen here. Make a story pole with markings that match the distance from the planned bottom of the excavation to the mason's line. Keep the lines in place as you dig (this does create an obstacle but it is the best way to assure that you don't overdig).

Excavate the patio site using the story pole as a depth guide. Be sure to call (in the U.S., simply dial "811") and have any utility lines flagged before you begin digging. Be careful not to dig too deeply, as the best base for your subbase is undisturbed earth. Once the excavation is complete, remove the strings and prepare for the installation of the subbase.

 ## CREATE A WHEELBARROW PATH

Create a temporary pathway from the subbase rock to the site using wood planks, old pavers, or any other surface you can create. This will minimize damage to your yard and make the heavy wheelbarrows safer to operate.

A permeable base is made with open-grade rock, which is simply landscape rock that has no fines or binders, as typical subbase (often called Class V or Class II) does. The bottom layer should be rock that is not smooth and has diameters of 1½" to 2" inches. Spread a 2-to 4"-deep layer of rock over the excavation area. Install a layer of landscape fabric over the site to inhibit weeds. Landscape fabric can be installed under the subbase or on top of the subbase, but must be under the setting base layer.

Spread the rock out into an even layer. Use a garden rake or landscape rake to spread it. The subbase should extend past the planned edges of the project area by at least 10" on all open sides.

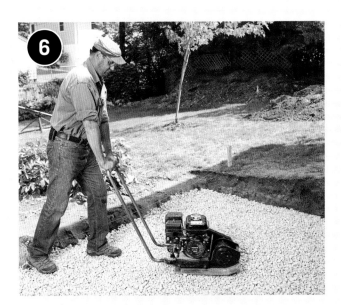

Tamp the rock to compact it. You can use a hand tamper, but for best results use a rented plate compactor. This is a very important part of creating a solid patio base. Compact the rock as you go: do not compact more than 2" of material at one time. Wear foam ear plugs or other ear protection.

Add additional layers of large rock until the base layer is at least 4" thick. Then, switch to a smaller open-grade rock for the next layer. Here, ¾" dia. buff limestone is being used. Add, spread and compact the smaller-grade rock until the leveled surface follows the grade of the patio and the surface of the rock layer is 2", plus the thickness of your surfacing material, below grade at the top of the worksite. This completes your permeable subbase. Add a sand setting layer and pavers according to the demands of your project.

Spaced Masonry Pavers

Safety glasses, gloves, ear protection	Trowel
Tape measure	Lengths of 1" metal conduit
Circular saw	Rigid paver edging, galvanized spikes
Hammer	Scrap plywood and 2× for making spacers
Drill driver, bits	
Excavation tools	¾ to 1½" open-grade stone for base
Stakes	
Mason's string	Coarse sand or screenings for setting bed
Line level	
Plate compactor	Pea gravel, river rock, or sand to fill gaps
Rubber mallet	
Rake	Topsoil (if adding plants)

A bit of space between each paver and its neighbor is all it takes to turn a mostly impervious surface like masonry pavers into a water-absorbing surface. Here are options for paver spacing gaps.

- **Spaced conventional pavers.** Install standard concrete pavers or bricks with several inches of between them. Fill the voids with river rock or creeping plants for water to drain easily.

- **Mounting grids.** Plastic mounting grids not only lock pavers in a consistent space from each other, they keep the installation smooth and level.

- **Pavers with preformed spacers.** Some pavers come with small nubs that separate them just enough to allow for drainage. They install as quickly and easily as conventional pavers.

For this project, you'll also need to prepare a deep substrate of coarse, angular gravel to handle the water. Your soil type will dictate its depth. At the extreme, you may have to excavate 10 to 12 inches to make room for 8 inches of ¾- to 1½-inch open-graded stone, followed by at least 2 inches of coarse sand as a setting bed.

The project that follows uses widely spaced 16-inch by 16-inch pavers. One advantage of large pavers is that they look best if laid out so only whole pieces are used. Once the substrate and edging is in place, use spacers and a taut line to install the pavers.

How to Install a Spaced-Paver Patio

Prepare a permeable subbase that extends at least 10" past the planned borders of the patio where possible. Install rigid paver edging around the border of the patio area to contain the coarse sand or crushed granite setting base material.

Embed 1"-dia. pieces of conduit into the sand at 4- to 6-ft. intervals, flush with one another and follow any slope you want to build into the patio). Scrape a piece of straight 2 × 4 along the conduit to level the paver setting medium. Slowly move the 2 × 4 back and forth in a sawing motion. Avoid walking on the setting bed once it is smooth. Remove the conduit and backfill the depressions.

Lay a setting bed at least 2" thick on top of the subbase. Level the setting bed. Do not use a power plate compactor on this bed, as it will make adjusting the pavers very difficult. Use a hand tamper to level things out and lightly compact the material.

Starting at a corner, set four tiles, using a cross spacer to position the pavers. Note: When using spacers to lay out a patio next to a house, always start at the house and work outward. In sites with a closed corner, choose that corner to start. If the corner is slightly out of square, you can make it up at the open sides of the patio where it is less noticeable.

(continued)

One of the least expensive ways to make an earth-friendly patio is to install conventional pavers with extra space between them for drainage. Any amount of spacing helps, whether a mere ¼-inch gap filled with coarse sand or 3 inches or more for stone or plantings. The consistent geometry of conventional pavers makes it relatively easy to achieve straight courses. However, once you introduce a gap you'll need to contrive spacers to help keep the gap consistent and the pavers neatly lined up. Guides can range from a few strips of ¼-inch hardboard to plywood combinations made to suit your arrangement.

Simple strips of ¼-inch hardboard or plywood work fine as gap guides. Adding a scrap of 1 × 2 makes them easier to use. Make several so they are always handy. This relatively small gap works well with smaller cast concrete pavers similar to brick pavers.

For a 1½-inch gap, use a 2 × 2 as a spacer. Adding a scrap of ½-inch plywood to ride on the paver tops makes the spacer easier to handle and helps you level adjacent pavers. This spacing is good with medium-sized pavers, such as these 8 × 16 concrete pavers.

To install a grid of square pavers, make a cross spacer about 16 inches by 16 inches. Two 2 × 2s gives you a roughly 3-inch gap without having to rip a 2 × 4. Add the cross made of ¼- to ¾-inch plywood to match to the thickness of the pavers and hold the 2 × 2s together. For ease of use, attach a 1 × 2 handle.

Continue setting pavers, outward from the corner. Once you've set several pavers, check to make sure they are level. Lay a straight 2 × 4 across the tops and look for gaps between the straightedge and the pavers.

OPTION: Fill gaps with topsoil or potting soil so you can add groundcover plants. Some may even add a pleasant fragrance as you walk across them. For areas with full sun, consider Creeping Thyme or Elfin Thyme. In partial sun, Goldmoss Sedum, Chamomile, Dichondra, and Irish Moss work well. In shady areas, go with Corsican Sandwort or Sweet Woodruff.

Add or remove bedding base from beneath the pavers as needed to bring them to level. Use some restraint here, as it is easy to throw off your layout by adding too much bedding.

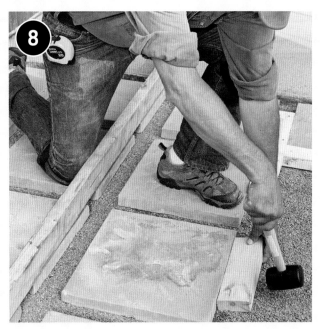

Use a rubber mallet and a scrap of 2 × 4 to adjust out-of-kilter pavers. Fill in between the pavers. Here, the crushed granite used in the base is added to fill in gaps. Keep extra on hand to refill gaps as needed.

Composite Permeable Pavers

Installing composite permeable pavers is a doubly conscientious way to surface your patio. Not only are you limiting runoff, you are saving energy by using pavers made mostly of scrap tires and plastics. The recycled materials keep the pavers light and easy to cut. In addition, installation is simplified because the pieces snap into a plastic grid—no bond line, setting, and resetting required. Patterns include herringbone, basket weave, or running bond. Wedge-shaped accessory pavers let you install curved borders.

As with any permeable material, you'll need to excavate deeply and add coarse gravel for adequate drainage. For a patio, dig down about 12 inches. Begin with a 6-inch layer of 2½-inch stone, compacted 2 inches at a time. Next add a 4-inch layer of 1-inch stone, topped off with a 2-inch bedding layer of ⅜-inch chip rock. Slope the final layers away from the house.

Before installation, choose a starting point. To give your project a squared-up start and reduce the amount of cutting you'll have to do, look for a corner on the longest straight edge.

TOOLS + MATERIALS

Safety glasses, gloves, ear protection	Hand compactor or vibrating plate compactor
Shovel	Jigsaw
Hand dolly	Power miter saw (optional)
Broom	¾- to 1½-inch open-grade stone for base
Straightedge or screed rake	
Hand trowel	Coarse sand or screenings for setting bed
Hammer	Pavers and setting grids
Tin snips	Legless and wedge pavers for curved border
Utility knife	
Edging and spikes	Caulk gun and exterior adhesive
4-foot level	

These pavers are not permeable themselves, but they fit onto a grid so they stay put while maintaining even gaps between units for good drainage. They can be installed as a resurfacing product over an old patio, or set onto a subbase like traditional paver products.

The installation grids on which these pavers are fitted allow water runoff to drain into the subbase as it filters down through the gaps between the composite paver units.

In general, recycled composite products weigh less than solid stone or wood, and because the size is uniform they can be laid in traditional paver patterns like basketweave or herringbone. The VAST pavers seen here (See Resources, page 238) come in five colors so you can incorporate color shifts into the layout pattern.

COMPOSITE PERMEABLE PAVERS

These AZEK pavers are made from 95% recycled material and fit into square grids that function like interlocking building blocks.

How to Install Composite Pavers

Create a smooth base for the installation as you would for a standard paver installation project. If you are working next to a concrete surface, notch a 2 × 4 so the thickness equals the height of the paver plus the grid and use the 2 × 4 to screed the setting layer smooth once it is compacted. Unlike sandset pavers, this product installs better if the base is compacted hard and smooth.

Lay out several grids on the bedding layer. These are held together by installing the pavers so they bridge the joints between the grids. Plan how to begin your pattern of choice—herringbone, basket weave, or running bond—so that at least one paver overlaps two grids in each direction.

Install the pavers, beginning in one corner and working across one side of the patio. Often the side along the house works best for starting to avoid having to cut too many pavers. Complete the field of the patio. Here, a basket weave pattern is being used. One advantage to the basket weave, compared to herringbone (inset), is that the basket weave does not require half-size pavers.

Use a charged hose (one with the water turned on but the sprayer off) to mark a curved edge, if your design calls for one. Lay out the curve and carefully mark it for cutting.

Cut the curved edge with a jigsaw equipped with a 5–6-tooth blade set just deep enough to cut through the pavers. You may need to attach a guide block to the foot of the saw to avoid cutting into the grids. But you can also cut the grids in place at the same time if you wish. Or, simply leave them and cover them with backfill. Note that any whole unused pavers can be easily lifted out and used elsewhere.

Use wedge-shaped pavers to create a decorative border treatment for the curve. Dry-fit the edge pavers first, since they are legless and do not lock into the installation grid. When satisfied, remove each piece.

Add beads of landscape block adhesive and reset the border pieces. Complete any straight edges in the same manner. Check with the product manufacturer first to see if they recommend a specific brand or type of adhesive.

Add edging, securing it with 10" galvanized spikes every foot or so. Trim the grid with a jigsaw or cover it with soil and turf. If you wish, sweep chip rock onto the surface before tamping the entire surface. Sweep additional rock into the cracks as you tamp. Chip rock, also called pulverized or decomposed granite, will fill the gaps and stabilize the surface without blocking water drainage.

Rubber Tile Patio

Rubber tiles are typically 18 or 24 inches square. For quick patio upgrades, tiles are generally an easier and less expensive option than recycled rubber pavers. Covering a patio with tiles couldn't be easier, and the resulting surface is maintenance free, aside from a quick hose-down to keep it clean. Because of the friction between rubber and concrete, the installation doesn't need perimeter edging to stay in place. The rubber material is also more comfortable underfoot than concrete and other hard surfaces—a nice feature for outdoor cooks who spend a lot of time standing at the grill. When choosing rubber tiles, look for products with good UV resistance and a nonslip, textured surface. Colors include brown, red, gray, tan, brick, blue, and green. Interlocking tiles and mats are a great solution for play areas when placed on compacted stone.

TOOLS + MATERIALS

Safety glasses, gloves, ear protection	Chalk line
Broom	Utility knife
Tape measure	Framing square
	Rubber mats or tiles

Some recycled rubber tiles interlock in some fashion, but most can simply be set in place. The weight of the tiles and the friction with the subsurface stabilizes them. As a final step some types are snugged together by clips linking the perimeter tiles.

How to Lay a Rubber Tile Patio

Create a layout for the installation by snapping one or more chalk lines for reference. Determine which edges of the patio will look best with full mats and which will have cut pieces. For the best effect, lay out the project so cut mats along the sides are roughly equal in size. When you're satisfied with the arrangement, snap a chalk line to guide the first row of mats at or near the patio's center.

Position tiles along the reference line, following the desired pattern. Complete any full-mat rows, such as along the house wall or front edge of the patio. Align the remaining mats, letting any cut rows run long until all of the mats are in place.

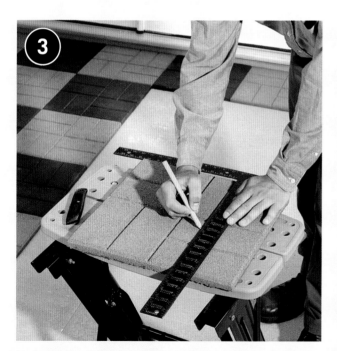

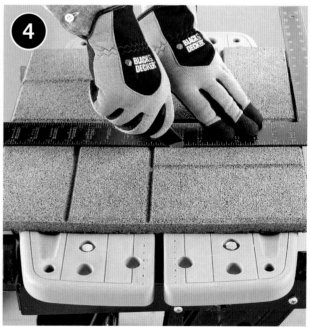

Mark the tiles for cutting using a straightedge like a framing square (shown) and a pencil.

Cut the mats with a sharp utility knife and a straightedge. Start with a careful scoring cut, then make a few more passes to cut through the material. Follow the manufacturer's instructions for installing the perimeter tiles.

Recycled Plastic Pavers

We discard in excess of 33 million tons of plastic each year. Too much of it winds up in landfills and waterways where it might take centuries to break down. Happily, recycled plastic is used to make composite decking, and, more recently, patio and walkway tiles. As with recycled rubber and glass, manufacturing these products requires less energy than concrete or brick products.

The system shown here has long been used as a pervious, non-cracking solution for sidewalks. Made of 100% recycled materials, the 2-inch-thick, 24- by 30-inch pavers weigh 35 pounds each. Each is molded with channels that hold the pavers off the subsurface to facilitate drainage.

The tiles come with tabs into which you pound spikes to hold them in place. The tabs also hold the tiles apart for adequate drainage. It most areas a 4-inch trench with 2 inches of aggregate is an adequate substrate.

TOOLS + MATERIALS

Safety glasses, gloves
Shovel
Hand dolly
Broom
Screed
Hammer
¼-inch spacers
4-foot level
Recycled plastic pavers, (See Resources, page 238)

Hand compactor or vibrating plate compactor
10-inch galvanized spikes
2 × 4s for temporary edging
Jigsaw
Permeable base material
Straightedge

How to Install a Plastic Paver Patio

Excavate for a minimum of 2" of ¾" angular gravel and a setting bed that allows for paver thickness. Soak and compact, add sand, and screed the surface smooth and level. Tip pavers in place so the tabs connect. Use ¼" spacers in the joints. Keep the spacers in place until all pavers are installed. Do your best to level each paver as you set it in place.

Make cutouts for trees or other irregular shapes using a jigsaw. Use a circular saw guided by a straightedge to make straight cuts in the pavers. Don't cut off the tabs around the outside edge—they help anchor the pavers.

Pound in 10" spikes through the center tab of each paver along the perimeter of the patio. The interlocking tabs hold the other pavers. Don't use more than one spike on any single paver edge.

Backfill with soil, stone, or concrete around the perimeter. The tabs are positioned low enough that they may be covered. You may also fill the gaps between pavers with chip rocks or other products that will not block drainage.

UPCYCLED CHIC

About 290 million tires are discarded each year, and most are recycled. Shredded rubber chips from tires makes for a comfortable, porous walkway or patio surface. Rubber chips can also be combined with stones and bound with a urethane binder. This can be blended on site in a cement mixer and laid in less time than brick pavers.

Recycled glass is also a good patio material when combined with a binder or concrete to fabricate pavers. The look is unique and the material is incredibly durable.

You won't find recycled glass pavers or rubber chip infill at most large home centers; you'll need to search for local specialty suppliers. However, these options can be well worth the search, combining environmentally friendly materials with low cost, durable alternatives to more traditional paving solutions.

Recycled rubber combined with stone using a urethane binder makes a smooth, seamless surface ideal for patios, walkways, and any horizontal surface.

Recycled glass combined with a bonding agent or concrete makes a colorful, long-lasting paver. Variations include square, rectangular, octagonal, and interlocking, in both a shiny or matte finish.

Thick, square tiles made from recycled glass and concrete are even more Earth-friendly if you lay them with gaps between tiles to allow drainage.

Before

After

Subsurface Grids

Homeowners who like the simplicity of a plain gravel patio often find that with time it becomes uneven. As the gravel compacts it becomes a home to puddles and damp areas—a great idea gone bad.

To conquer this problem—and create a truly permeable patio—consider installing subsurface mats. Made with linked plastic rings roughly 1-inch tall, they hold gravel in place while adding compressive strength. That not only improves the appearance of the surface but also significantly strengthens it so it can bear any amount of patio traffic. Landscaping fiber adhered to the bottom of the mat keeps particles from clogging the subsurface, preserving its ability to drain.

But beyond that, the quality of the loose rock surface created with this system is smooth and comfortable enough that you can park cars on the surface when it is not being used as a patio. Then, when it's time for that graduation party or Memorial Day blowout, replace the cars with patio furnishings and your satellite patio is ready to go.

The mats we used for this project are called Gravelpave (See resources, page 236) and they come in rolls as small as 3½ feet wide by 33 feet long. At 108 square feet, that's just enough for a 10 by 10-foot patio. Colors include tan, gray, terracotta, and black to match the primary tone of the surfacing rock.

As with any permeable surface, you'll need to excavate to create a deep enough gravel base to handle the accumulated water. Most importantly, you'll need to use stone that is small (about $3/16$-inch), washed, angular, and hard. Pea gravel won't cut it—it tends to roll around or bounce out.

Once the mat and appropriate gravel are installed, the only maintenance is an occasional sweeping with a push broom or leaf blower. The rings may show through slightly after time. Add and compact more gravel as needed.

Opposite: Do you have an unpaved parking area that is next to your yard? Convert it into an overflow patio area for entertaining by eliminating ruts and soft spots with a subsurface grid and some fresh rock.

TOOLS + MATERIALS

Safety glasses, gloves	Hand compactor or vibrating plate compactor
Excavation tools	
4-ft. level	10" galvanized spikes (with ring shanks)
Broom	
Tin snips	Permeable base material
Utility knife	Straightedge
Hammer	Jackhammer (optional)

Subsurface mats add compressive strength to gravel in areas of heavy use. Ideal as permeable surfaces on patios or play areas, the mats install quickly and require minimal maintenance. The plastic rings contain loose gravel fill so it doesn't scatter or become rutted.

How to Install a Gravel Patio with Subsurface Grids

Start digging (be sure to call 811 first to check for underground lines). To get an adequate layer of drainage rock you'll need to go down at least 8".

OPTION: If you are installing the grid over an area previously used for parking, the ground is likely to be extremely dense and compacted. The money it costs to rent a jackhammer is well worth the investment. Ask for a spade bit or a clay bit.

Install the layer of drainage rock. Here, a 6"-thick layer of ¾"-diameter buff limestone is being compacted with a plate compactor. Be sure to get open-grade rock with no fines. If you are working near a street or alley, you can probably have the rock dumped right into the excavation site.

Unroll the subsurface grid onto the thoroughly compacted drainage rock. The strips are manufactured with male and female tabs along the edges so they can snap together, so mind the alignment of the strips.

Cut the strips to length using aviator snips or pruning shears to cut through the plastic matrix. Use a utility knife to slice through the landscape textile.

Snap adjoining strips together. The male and female fittings at the edges are easy to lock together securely by pressing down on the connection with a $3/8$" or $1/2$" nut driver or socket. Slipping a long backer board underneath the seam first helps.

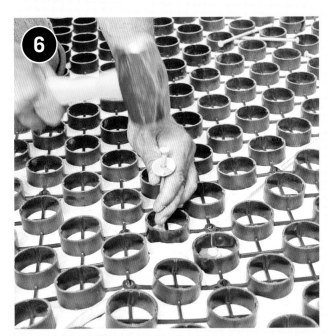

Anchor the gravel mat using 10" spikes fitted with washers pounded in every sixth ring. Put some extra spikes in along edges and at high traffic areas. If you can find them, look for spikes with a ring shank to help prevent them from working loose in the rock base. If you will be using edging around the perimeter to contain the gravel, install it now.

Topdress with gravel. Fill the area so the gravel is at least $1/4$" above the tops of the rings. Be sure to use $3/16$" gravel that is angular and hard. It is normal that the rings show slightly, but if you over fill slightly this will be minimized. Settle the gravel by tamping with a plate compactor.

Walkways + Steps

A walkway or path can do much more than provide a route for foot traffic. A path can be a versatile design element, creating an attractive border along a house, a patio, or landscape features. It can also become an attractive transition between two areas, such as a lawn and a planting bed.

Walkways and paths are also effective at unifying spaces in the landscape. For example, imagine a backyard with a patio at one end, a beautiful flower garden at the other, and a solid swath of lawn in-between. By adding a footpath, you connect all of the areas.

In terms of construction techniques and material, a walkway is essentially a patio in a different configuration. All of the same materials that make great patio surfaces are equally as suitable for walkways. In this chapter, you'll find complete projects utilizing all major walkway materials, plus some you might not have thought of. You'll also find a special section with tips for planning your walkway project and laying out the site.

In This Chapter:

- Designing Walkways + Steps
- Sandset Brick Walkway
- Poured Concrete Walkway
- Decorative Concrete Path
- Flagstone Walkway
- Simple Gravel Path
- Pebbled Stepping Stone Path
- Timber Garden Steps
- Flagstone Garden Steps

Designing Walkways + Steps

Designing and planning a new walkway starts with a careful assessment of how the path will be used. Landscape designers commonly group outdoor walkways into three main categories, according to use and overall design goals.

The first is a *primary walkway*: a high-traffic path used by household members and visitors, such as a walkway between the street and the home's main entry door. A main path should provide the quickest and easiest route from point A to point B. Any unnecessary twists and turns are likely to be cross-cut by walkers, leaving you with a less manicured path through the yard. To allow two people to walk side-by-side, a main path should be 42 to 48 inches wide. Surface materials should be durable, slip-resistant, and easy to shovel (if you live in a snowy climate), such as poured concrete, pavers, or flat stones.

A *secondary walkway* typically connects the house to a patio or outbuilding or a patio to a well-used area in the yard. A comfortable width for single-person travel is 24 to 36 inches. Surfaces should be flat and level underfoot and provide good drainage and slip-resistance in all seasons.

The third type, a *tertiary path*, is informal, perhaps nothing more than a line of stepping stones meandering through a flower garden or a simple gravel path leading to a secluded seating area. Design tertiary paths for a comfortable stride, with a minimum width of 12 to 16 inches.

Once you've established the design criteria for your walkway or path, spend some time testing the size and configuration of the route to be sure it will meet your needs. See page 141 for help with planning a set of stairs for your walkway or landscape.

As an important part of a home's curb appeal, a primary walkway should be styled to complement the house exterior and street-side landscaping.

Secondary walkways can be a blend of practicality and decoration. A gentle curve here and there adds interest without slowing travel too much.

A tertiary path can be as rustic or creative as you like. It can serve as an invitation to stroll through a garden or an access path for tending plants—or both.

TOOLS + MATERIALS

Stakes	Marking paint
Mason's string	Lumber (1 × 2,
Maul	1 × 4, 2 × 4)
Plate compactor	Level
Compactable gravel	Drill and bits
Excavation tools	Cardboard
Line level	Screws
¾" rope	Eye protection
	Work gloves

How to Lay Out a Straight Walkway

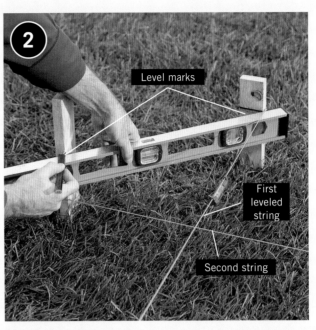

Use temporary stakes and mason's string to plan the walkway layout. Drive stakes at the ends of each section and at any corners, then tie the strings to the stakes to represent the edges of the finished path. Run a second set of strings 6" outside the first lines.

Set up a new string layout to mark the precise borders of the finished walkway. Along the high edge of the walkway, set the strings to the finished surface height. Use a line level to make sure the strings are level. *Tip: For 90° turns, use the 3-4-5 technique to set the strings accurately at 90°.*

Set the border strings lower for the slope. The finished surface follows a downward slope of ¼" per foot on the opposite side of the walkway. Use a homemade slope gauge to set the height of the strings. Fine-tune the gravel base to follow the slope setting, and prepare for the sand bed and/or surface material.

Excavate the area within the string lines. First, cut sod along the inside edge of the second string line. Remove all grass and plantings from the excavation area. Add the gravel subbase.

Experiment with different sizes and shapes for the walkway using two lengths of ¾" braided rope or a garden hose. To maintain a consistent width, cut spacers from 1 × 2 lumber and use them to set the spacing between the rope outlines.

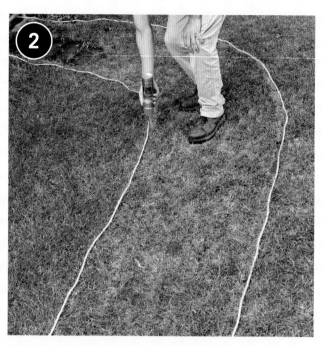

Mark the ground with marking paint, following the final outline of the ropes. Excavate the area 6" beyond the marked outline (or as required for your choice of edging.) If desired, you can set up a string layout to guide the installation of the gravel subbase.

Create a slope gauge for checking the slope of your gravel base, edging, or surface material. Tape a level and a drill bit to a straight 2 × 4 that's a little longer than the width of the walkway. The slope should be ¼" per foot: for a 2-ft. level, use a ½"-dia. bit or spacer; for a 4-ft. level, use a 1"-thick spacer. The slope is correct when the board is level.

 PLANNING A STEPPING STONE PATH

To plan a simple stepping stone path, cut pieces of cardboard to roughly the same size as an average stone you're using. Lay out the pieces in the desired route, then walk along the "stones" to make sure the spacing is comfortable for walking with a casual stride. Leave the test pieces in place to guide the excavation and/or stone setting.

How to Plan Landscape Steps

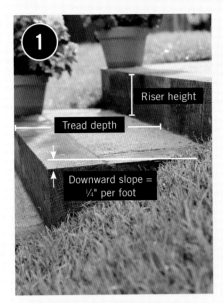

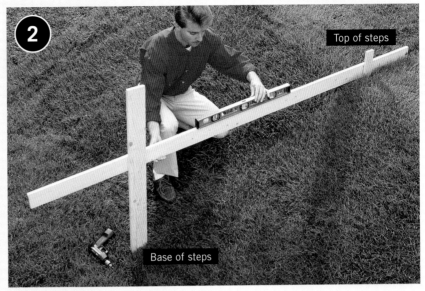

Landscape steps are best with a riser height (vertical dimension) of 6" or less and a tread depth (horizontal dimension) of 11" or more. Plan to build each tread with a downward slope of ¼" per foot from back to front. Complete the following steps to calculate the tread and riser dimensions for your steps.

Drive a tall stake into the ground at the base of the stairway site. Adjust the stake so it is perfectly plumb. Drive a shorter stake at the top of the site. Position a long, straight 1 × 4 or 2 × 4 against the stakes, with one end touching the ground next to the top stake. Adjust the 1 × 4 so it is level, then attach it to the stakes with screws. For long spans, use a mason's string instead of a board.

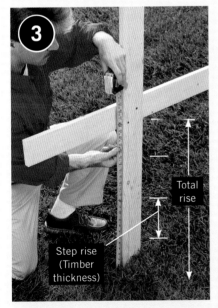

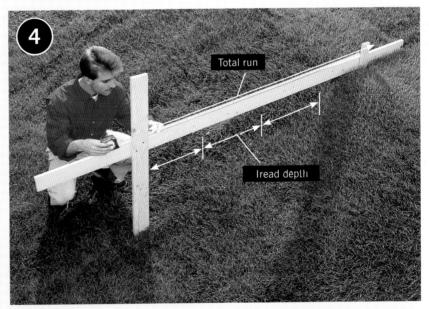

Measure from the ground to the bottom of the 1 × 4 to find the total rise of the stairway. Divide the total rise by the desired riser height to find the number of steps you need. If the result contains a fraction, drop the fraction and divide the rise by the whole number to find the exact riser dimension.

Measure along the 1 × 4 between the stakes to find the total horizontal run of the stairway. Divide the total run by the number of steps to find the depth of each step tread. If the depth is less than 11", revise the step layout to extend the depth of the treads.

Sandset Brick Walkway

Sandset brick is a good choice of material for a walkway for the same reasons that make it a great patio surface—it's easy to work with, it lends itself equally well to traditional paving patterns and creative custom designs, and it can be installed at a leisurely pace because there's no mortar or wet concrete involved. The timeless look of natural clay brick is especially well-suited to walkways, where the rhythmic patterns of geometric lines create a unique sense of movement that draws your eye down the path toward its destination.

In this walkway project, all of the interior (*field*) bricks are arranged in the installation area and then the curving side edges of the walk are marked onto the set bricks to ensure perfect cutting lines. After the edge bricks are cut and reset, border bricks are installed followed by rigid paver edging to keep everything in place. This is the most efficient method for installing a curving path. Straight walkways can follow the standard process of installing the edging and border bricks (on one or both sides of the path, as applicable) before laying the field brick, as is done in the brick patio project.

With standard brick, you'll need to set the gaps with spacers cut from ⅛-inch hardboard, as shown in this project.

TOOLS + MATERIALS

Tape measure	1 × 2 lumber
¾" braided rope	Compactable gravel
Marking paint	Straight 2 × 4
Excavation tools	Duct tape
Plate compactor	Coarse sand
Mason's string	Landscape fabric
Stakes	Landscape staples
Hand tamp	Brick paver units
2- or 4-ft. level	Plastic patio edging
Drill bits	⅛" hardboard
Rubber mallet	Paver joint sand
Straightedge	Eye protection
Trowel	Work gloves
Masonry saw	12" galvanized spikes
Push broom	Maul

A curving brick walkway can be as much a design statement as a course for easy travel. Curves require more time than straight designs, due to the extra cutting involved, but the results can be all the more stunning.

How to Install a Sandset Brick Walkway

Lay out the walkway curved edges using ¾" braided rope (or use mason's strings for straight sections. Cut 1 × 2 or 2 × 2 spacers to the desired path width and then place them in-between the ropes for consistent spacing. Mark the outlines along the inside edges of the ropes onto the ground with marking paint.

Excavate the area 6" outside of the marked lines along both sides of the path. Remove soil to allow for a 4"-thick subbase of gravel, a 1" layer of sand, and the thickness of the brick pavers (minus the height of the finished paving above the ground). The finished paving typically rests about 1" aboveground for ease of lawn maintenance. Thoroughly tamp the area with a plate compactor.

Spread out an even layer of compactable gravel—enough for a 4"-thick layer after compaction. Grade the gravel to follow a downward slope of ¼" per foot (most long walkways slope from side to side, while shorter paths or walkway sections can be sloped along their length). Use a homemade slope gauge to screed the gravel smooth and to check the slope as you work (see step 3, page 141). Tamp the subbase thoroughly with the plate compactor, making sure the surface is flat and smooth and properly sloped.

(continued)

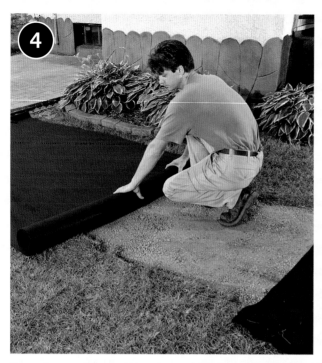

Cover the gravel base with professional-grade landscape fabric, overlapping the strips by at least 6". If desired, tack the fabric in place with landscape staples.

Spread a 1" layer of coarse sand over the landscape fabric. Screed the sand with a board so it is smooth, even, and flat.

Tamp the screeded sand with a hand tamper or a plate compactor. Check the slope of the surface as you go.

Spacer

Begin the paving at one end of the walkway, following the desired pattern. Use ⅛"-thick hardboard spacers in-between the bricks to set the sand-joint gaps. *Tip: It's best to start the paving against a straightedge or square corner. If your walkway does not connect to a patio or stoop, set a temporary 2 × 4 with stakes at the end of the walkway to create a straight starting line.*

Option: If your walkway includes long straight sections between curves, set up guidelines with stakes and mason's strings to keep the ends of the courses straight as you pave.

Set the next few courses of brick, running them long over the side edges. With the first few courses in place, tap the bricks with a rubber mallet to bed them into the sand.

Lay out the curved edges of the finished walkway using ¾" braided rope . Adjust the ropes as needed so that the cut bricks will be roughly symmetrical on both edges of the walkway. Also measure between the ropes to make sure the finished width will be accurate according to your layout. Trace along the ropes with a pencil to mark the cutting lines onto the bricks.

(continued)

Variation: Cut field bricks after installing the edging. Mark each brick for cutting by holding it in position and drawing the cut line across the top face.

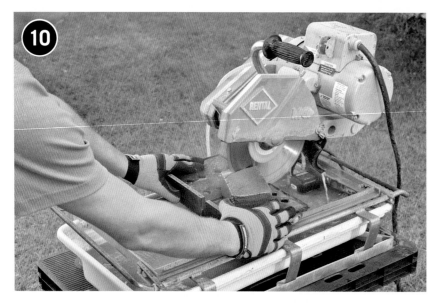

Cut the bricks with a rented masonry saw (wet saw), following the instructions from the tool supplier. Make straight cuts with a single, full-depth cut. Curved cuts require multiple straight cuts made tangentially to the cutting line. After cutting a brick, reset it before cutting the next brick.

Align the border bricks (if applicable) snug against the edges of the field paving. Use a straightedge or level to make sure the border units are flush with the tops of the field bricks. Set the border bricks with a rubber mallet. Dampen the exposed edges of the sand bed, and then use a trowel to slice away the edge so it's flush with the paving.

Install rigid paver edging (bendable) or other edge material tight against the outside of the walkway.

Fill and tamp the sand joints one or more times until the joints are completely filled. Sweep up any loose sand.

Soak the surface with water and let it dry. Cover the edging sides with soil and sod or other material, as desired.

Poured Concrete Walkway

If you've always wanted to try your hand at creating with concrete, an outdoor walkway is a great project to start with. The basic elements and construction steps of a walkway are similar to those of a poured concrete patio or other landscape slab, but the smaller scale of a walkway makes it a much more manageable project for first-timers. Placing the wet concrete goes faster, and you can easily reach the center of the surface for finishing from either side of the walkway.

Like a patio slab, a poured concrete walkway also makes a good foundation for mortared surface materials, like pavers, stone, and tile. If that's your goal, be sure to account for the thickness of the surface material when planning and laying out the walkway height. A coarse broomed or scratched finish on the concrete will help create a strong bond with the mortar bed of the surface material.

The walkway in this project is a 4-inch-thick by 26-inch-wide concrete slab with a broom finish for slip resistance. It consists of two straight, 12-ft.-long runs connected by a 90° elbow. After curing, the walkway can be left bare for a classic, low-maintenance surface, or it can be colored with a permanent acid stain. When planning your walkway project, consult your city's building department for recommendations and construction requirements.

TOOLS + MATERIALS

Drill, bits	$\frac{7}{16}$" hardboard siding
Circular saw	Compactable gravel
Mason's string	6 × 6" 10/10 welded wire mesh (wwm)
Line level	
Excavation tools	Tie wire
2- or 4-ft. level	2" bolsters
Plate compactor	Isolation board and construction adhesive
Heavy-duty wire cutters or bolt cutters	Release agent
Concrete mixing tools	4,000 psi concrete (or as required by local code)
Shovel	Clear polyethylene sheeting
Hammer	
Magnesium float	Eye protection
Edger tool	Work gloves
Groover tool	4" deck screws
Magnesium trowel	#3 rebar (optional)
Push broom	Wood stakes
Lumber (2 × 2, 2 × 4)	Tape measure
Drywall screws (2½", 3½")	

Poured concrete walkways can be designed with straight lines, curves, or any angles you desire. The flat, hardwearing surface is ideal for frequently traveled paths and will stand up to heavy equipment and decades of snow shoveling.

Sloping a Walkway

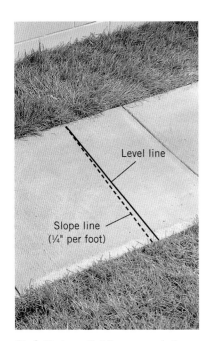

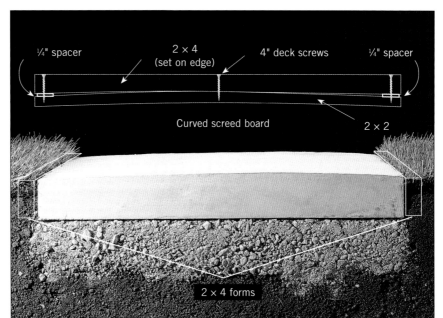

Straight slope: Set the concrete form lower on one side of the walk-way so the finished surface is flat and slopes downward at a rate of ¼" per foot. Always slope the surface away from the house foundation or, when not near the house, toward the area best suited to accept water runoff.

Crowned slope: When a walkway does not run near the house foundation, you have the option of crowning the surface so it slopes down to both sides. To make the crown, construct a curved screed board by cutting a 2 × 2 and a 2 × 4 long enough to rest on both sides of the concrete form. Sandwich the boards together with a ¼"-thick spacer at each end, then fasten the assembly with 4" deck screws driven at the center and the ends. Use the board to screed the concrete).

Reinforcing a Walkway

As an alternative to the wire mesh reinforcement used in the following project, you can reinforce a walkway slab with metal rebar (check with the local building code requirements). For a 3-ft.-wide walkway, lay two sections of #3 rebar spaced evenly inside the concrete form. Bend the rebar as needed to follow curves or angles. Overlap pieces by 12" and tie them together with tie wire. Use wire bolsters to suspend the bar in the middle of the slab's thickness.

Lay out the precise edges of the finished walkway using stakes (or batterboards) and mason's string. Where possible, set stakes 12" or so outside of the walkway edges so they're out of the way. Make sure any 90° corners are square using the 3-4-5 measuring technique. Level the strings, then lower the strings on one side of the layout to create a downward slope of ¼" per foot (if the walkway will be crowned instead of sloped to one side, keep all strings level with one another. Cut away the sod or other plantings 6" beyond the layout lines on all sides of the site.

Excavate the site for a 4- to 6"-thick gravel subbase, plus any subgrade (below ground level) portion of the slab, as desired. Measure the depth with a story pole against the high-side layout strings, then use a slope gauge (see page 141) to grade the slope. Tamp the soil thoroughly with a plate compactor.

Cover the site with a 4- to 6"-layer of gravel and screed the surface flat, checking with a slope gauge to set the proper grade. Compact the gravel so the top surface is 4" below the finished walkway height. Reset the layout strings at the precise height of the finished walkway.

Build the concrete form with straight 2 × 4 lumber so the inside faces of the form are aligned with the strings. Drive 2 × 4 stakes for reinforcement behind butt joints. Align the form with the layout strings, and then drive stakes at each corner and every 2 to 3 ft. in between. Fasten the form to the stakes so the top inside corner of the form boards are just touching the layout strings. The tops of the stakes should be just below the tops of the form.

Add curved strips made from ¼- to ⅜"-thick plywood hardboard or lauan to create curved corners, if desired. Secure curved strips by screwing them to wood stakes. Recheck the gravel bed inside the concrete form, making sure it is smooth and properly sloped.

Lay reinforcing wire mesh over the gravel base, keeping the edges 1 to 2" from the insides of the form. Overlap the mesh strips by 6" (one square) and tie them together with tie wire. Prop up the mesh on 2" bolsters placed every few feet and tied to the mesh with wire. Install isolation board where the walkway adjoins other slabs or structures. When you're ready for the concrete pour, coat the insides of the form with a release agent or vegetable oil.

Drop the concrete in pods, starting at the far end of the walkway. Distribute it around the form by placing it (don't throw it) with a shovel. As you fill, stab into the concrete with the shovel, and tap a hammer against the back sides of the form to eliminate air pockets. Continue until the form is evenly filled, slightly above the tops of the form.

(continued)

Immediately screed the surface with a straight 2 × 4: two people pull the board backward in a side-to-side sawing motion with the board resting on top of the form. As you work, shovel in extra concrete to fill low spots or remove concrete from high spots, and re-screed. The goal is to create a flat surface that's level with the top of the form.

Float the concrete surface with a magnesium float, working back and forth in broad arching strokes. Tip up the leading edge of the tool slightly to prevent gouging the surface. Stop floating once the surface is relatively smooth and has a wet sheen. Be careful not to over-float, indicated by water pooling on the surface. Allow the bleed water to disappear and the concrete to harden sufficiently.

Use an edger to shape the side edges of the walkway along the wood form. Carefully run the edger back and forth along the form to create a smooth, rounded corner, lifting the leading edge of the tool slightly to prevent gouging.

Mark the locations of the control joints onto the top edges of the form boards, spacing the joints at intervals 1½ times the width of the walkway.

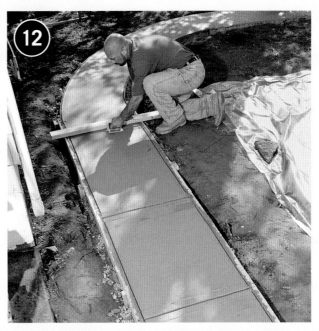

Cut the control joints with a 1" groover guided by a straight 2 × 4 held (or fastened) across the form at the marked locations. Make several light passes back and forth until the groove reaches full depth, lifting the leading edge of the tool to prevent gouging. Remove the guide board once each joint is complete. If desired, smooth out the marks made by the groover using a magnesium trowel.

Create a nonslip surface with a broom finish: starting at the far side edge of the walkway, steadily drag a broom backward over the surface in a straight line using a single pulling motion. Repeat in single, parallel passes (with minimal or no overlap), and rinse off the broom bristles after each pass. The stiffer and coarser the broom, the rougher the texture will be.

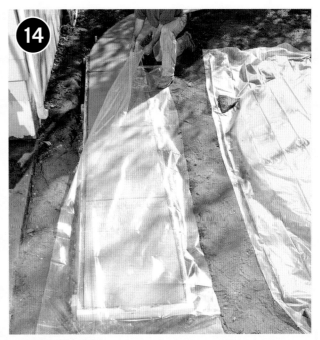

Cure the concrete by misting the walkway with water, then covering it with clear polyethylene sheeting. Smooth out any air pockets (which can cause discoloration), and weight down the sheeting along the edges. Mist the surface and reapply the plastic daily for 1 to 2 weeks.

Decorative Concrete Path

A well-made walkway or garden path not only stands up to years of hard use, it enhances the natural landscape and complements a home's exterior features. While traditional walkway materials like brick and stone have always been prized for both appearance and durability, most varieties are quite pricey and often difficult to install. As an easy and inexpensive alternative, you can build a new concrete path using manufactured forms. The result is a beautiful pathway that combines the custom look of brick or natural stone with all the durability and economy of poured concrete.

Laying this type of a path is a great do-it-yourself project. Once you've laid out the path, you mix the concrete, set and fill the form, then lift off the form to reveal the finished design. After a little troweling to smooth the surfaces, you're ready to create the next section—using the same form. Simply repeat the process until the path is complete. Each form creates a section that's approximately two square feet using one 80-lb. bag of premixed concrete. This project shows you all the basic steps for making any length of pathway, plus special techniques for making curves, adding a custom finish, or coloring the concrete to suit your personal design.

TOOLS + MATERIALS

Excavation and site preparation tools	Work gloves
Concrete mold	Liquid concrete colorant
Wheelbarrow or mixing box	Clear polyethylene sheeting
Shovel	Polymer-modified jointing sand or mortar mix
Margin trowel or concrete finishing trowel	Compactable gravel (optional)
Fiber-reinforced concrete mix	Level
	Broom or stiff brush

Basketweave Brick

Country Stone Pattern

Running Bond Brick

European Block Brick

Concrete path molds are available in a range of styles and decorative patterns. Coloring the wet concrete is a great way to add a realistic look to the path design.

How to Create a Straight or 90° Decorative Concrete Path

Prepare the project site by leveling the ground, removing sod or soil as needed. For a more durable base, excavate the area and add 2 to 4" of compactable gravel. Grade and compact the gravel layer so it is level and flat. See pages 43 to 47 for detailed steps on layout and site preparation.

Mix a batch of concrete for the first section, following the product directions. Place the form at the start of your path and level it, if desired. Shovel the wet concrete into the form to fill each cavity. Consolidate and smooth the surface of the form using a concrete margin trowel.

Promptly remove the form, and then trowel the edges of the section to create the desired finish (it may help to wet the trowel in water). For a nonslip surface, broom the section or brush it with a stiff brush. Place the form against the finished section and repeat steps 2 and 3 to complete the next section.

After removing each form, remember to trowel the edges of the section to create the desired finish. Repeat until the path is finished. If desired, rotate the form 90° with each section to vary the pattern. Cure the path by covering it with polyethylene sheeting for 5 to 7 days, lifting the plastic and misting the concrete with water each day.

(continued)

⑤

Fill walkway joints with sand or mortar mix to mimic the look of hand-laid stone or brick. Sweep the sand or dry mortar into the section contours and spaces between sections. For mortar, mist the joints with water so they harden in place.

Create custom surface finishes by pressing small stones or pea gravel into the wet concrete or by brushing on a layer of sand. Apply finish materials after the concrete has reached its initial set (thumb print hard) but is still damp—approximately one hour after placing.

COLORING YOUR CONCRETE

Adding colorant to the concrete mix is the easiest method and produces consistent results:

1. Combine liquid concrete colorant with water and mix into each bag-quantity of dry concrete mix, following the manufacturer's instructions. Blend thoroughly for consistent coloring, then add clean water to the mix, as needed, to achieve the proper consistency for pouring the concrete.

2. After placing and finishing the path sections, cure the concrete carefully to produce the best color quality. If curing conditions will be less than ideal, apply concrete sealer to ensure slow, even curing and good coloring.

Coloring gives molded concrete a more natural-looking finish and is great for blending your path or walkway into your landscape design.

How to Lay a Curved Decorative Concrete Path

After removing the form from a freshly poured section reposition the form in the direction of the curve and press down to slice off the inside corner of the section (photo left). Trowel the cut edge (and the rest of the section) to finish. Pour the next section following the curve (photo right). Cut off as many sections as needed to complete the curve. Cure the path by covering it with plastic sheeting for 5 to 7 days, lifting the plastic and misting the concrete with water each day.

Sprinkle the area around the joint or joints between pavers with polymer-modified jointing sand after the concrete has cured sufficiently so that the sand does not adhere. Sweep the product into the gap to clean the paver surfaces while filling the gap.

Mist the jointing sand with clean water, taking care not to wash the sand out of the joint. Once the water dries, the polymers in the mixture will have hardened the sand to look like a mortar joint. Refresh as needed.

Flagstone Walkway

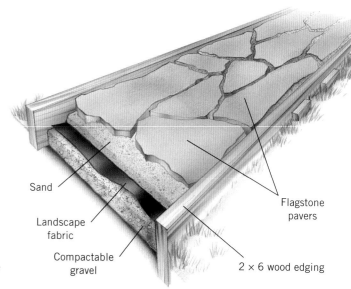

Sand

Landscape fabric

Compactable gravel

Flagstone pavers

2 × 6 wood edging

Natural flagstone is an ideal material for creating landscape floors. It's attractive and durable and blends well with both formal and informal landscapes. Although flagstone structures are often mortared, they can also be constructed with the sand-set method. Sand-setting flagstones is much faster and easier than setting them with mortar.

There are a variety of flat, thin sedimentary rocks that can be used for this project. Home and garden stores often carry several types of flagstone, but stone supply yards usually have a greater variety. Some varieties of flagstone cost more than others, but there are many affordable options. When you buy the flagstone for your project, select pieces in a variety of sizes from large to small. Arranging the stones for your walkway is similar to putting together a puzzle, and you'll need to see all the pieces laid out.

The following example demonstrates how to build a straight flagstone walkway with wood edging. If you'd like to build a curved walkway, select another edging material, such as brick or cut stone. Instead of filling gaps between stones with sand, you might want to fill them with topsoil and plant grass or some other ground cover between the stones.

TOOLS + MATERIALS

Excavation tools	Sand
Circular saw with masonry blade	2 × 6 pressure-treated lumber
Power drill	Deck screws
Masonry chisel	Compactable gravel
Maul	Flagstone pavers
Rubber mallet	Eye protection
Landscape fabric	Work gloves

Flagstone walkways combine durability with beauty and work well for casual or formal landscapes.

How to Build a Flagstone Walkway

Lay out, excavate, and prepare the base for the walkway. Form edging by installing 2 × 6 pressure-treated lumber around the perimeter of the pathway. Drive stakes on the outside of the edging, spaced 12" apart. The tops of the stakes should be below ground level. Drive galvanized screws through the edging and into the stakes.

Test-fit the stones over the walkway base, finding an attractive arrangement that limits the number of cuts needed. The gaps between the stones should range between ⅜ and 2" wide. Use a pencil to mark the stones for cutting, then remove the stones and place them beside the walkway in the same arrangement. Score along the marked lines with a circular saw and masonry blade set to ⅛" blade depth. Set a piece of wood under the stone, just inside the scored line. Use a masonry chisel and maul to strike along the scored line until the stone breaks.

Lay overlapping strips of landscape fabric over the walkway base and spread a 2"-layer of sand over it. Make a screed board from a short 2 × 6, notched to fit inside the edging. Pull the screed from one end of the walkway to the other, adding sand as needed to create a level base.

Beginning at one corner of the walkway, lay the flagstones onto the sand base. Repeat the arrangement you created in step 2, with ⅜- to 2"-wide gaps between stones. If necessary, add or remove sand to level the stones, then set them by tapping them with a rubber mallet or a length of 2 × 4.

Fill the gaps between the stones with sand. (Use topsoil if you're going to plant grass or ground cover between the stones.) Pack sand into the gaps, then spray the entire walkway with water to help settle the sand. Repeat until the gaps are completely filled and tightly packed with sand.

Loose materials can be used as filler between solid surface materials, like flagstone, or laid as the primary ground cover, as shown here.

Simple Gravel Path

Loose-fill gravel pathways are perfect for stone gardens, casual yards, and other situations where a hard surface is not required. The material is inexpensive, and its fluidity accommodates curves and irregular edging. Since gravel may be made from any rock, gravel paths may be matched to larger stones in the environment, tying them in to your landscaping. The gravel you choose need not be restricted to stone, either. Industrial and agricultural byproducts, such as cinder and ashes, walnut shells, recycled rubber chips, and ceramic fragments may also be used as path material.

For a more stable path, choose angular or jagged gravel over rounded materials. However, if your preference is to stroll throughout your landscape barefoot, your feet will be better served with smoother stones, such as river rock or pond pebbles. With stone, look for a crushed product in the ¼-to ¾-inch range. Angular or smooth, stones smaller than that can be tracked into the house, while larger materials are uncomfortable and potentially hazardous to walk on. If it complements your landscaping, use light-colored gravel, such as buff limestone. Visually, it is much easier to follow a light pathway at night because it reflects more moonlight.

Stable edging helps keep the pathway gravel from migrating into the surrounding mulch and soil. When integrated with landscape fabric, the edge keeps invasive perennials and trees from sending roots and shoots into the path. Do not use gravel paths near plants and trees that produce messy fruits, seeds, or other debris that will be difficult to remove from the gravel. Organic matter left on gravel paths will eventually rot into compost that will support weed growth.

A base of compactable gravel under the surface material keeps the pathway firm underfoot. For best results, embed the surface gravel material into the paver base with a plate compactor. This prevents the base from showing through if the gravel at the surface is disturbed. An underlayment of landscape fabric helps stabilize the pathway and blocks weeds, but if you don't mind pulling an occasional dandelion and are building on firm soil, it can be omitted.

TOOLS + MATERIALS

Mason's string	Straight 2 × 4
Hose or rope	Edging
Marking paint	Spikes
Excavation tools	Professional-grade
Garden rake	landscape fabric
Plate compactor	Compactable gravel
Sod stripper or power sod cutter	Dressed gravel
	Eye and ear protection
Wood stakes	Work gloves
Lumber (1 × 2, 2 × 4)	Circular saw
	Maul

Construction Details

Staked metal edging separates dirt from gravel

2+ inches of gravel forms the walking surface

Grade

Grade

Landscape fabric overlaps edging to keep out roots and rhizomes

2+ inches of paver base forms a bed for the walking surface

To ensure that the edges of the pathway are exactly parallel, create a spacer bar and use it as a guide to install the edging. Start with a piece of 2 × 4 that's a bit longer than the path width. Near one end, cut a notch that will fit snugly over the edging. Trim the spacer so the distance from the notch to the other end is the planned width of the pathway.

How to Lay a Gravel Pathway

Lay out one edge of the path excavation. Use a section of hose or rope to create curves, and use stakes and string to indicate straight sections). Cut 1 × 2 spacers to set the path width and establish the second pathway edge; use another hose and/or more stakes and string to lay out the other edge. Mark both edges with marking paint.

Remove sod in the walkway area using a sod stripper or a power sod cutter (see option, at right). Excavate the soil to a depth of 4 to 6". Measure down from a 2 × 4 placed across the path bed to fine-tune the excavation. Grade the bottom of the excavation flat using a garden rake. *Note: If mulch will be used outside the path, make the excavation shallower by the depth of the mulch.* Compact the soil with a plate compactor.

Option: Use a power sod cutter to strip grass from your pathway site. Available at most rental centers and large home centers, sod cutters excavate to a very even depth. The cut sod can be replanted in other parts of your lawn.

Lay landscaping fabric from edge to edge, lapping over the undisturbed ground on either side of the path. On straight sections, you may be able to run parallel to the path with a single strip; on curved paths, it's easier to lay the fabric perpendicular to the path. Overlap all seams by 6".

Install edging over the fabric. Shim the edging with small stones, if necessary, so the top edge is ½" above grade (if the path passes through grass) or 2" above grade (if it passes through a mulched area). Secure the edging with spikes. To install the second edge, use a 2 × 4 spacer gauge that's been notched to fit over your edging.

Stone or vertical-brick edges may be set in deeper trenches at the sides of the path. Place these on top of the fabric also. You do not have to use additional edging with paver edging, but metal (or other) edging will keep the pavers from wandering.

(continued)

Trim excess fabric, then backfill behind the edging with dirt and tamp it down carefully with the end of a 2 × 4. This secures the edging and helps it to maintain its shape.

Add a 2- to 4"-thick layer of compactable gravel over the entire pathway. Rake the gravel flat. Then, spread a thin layer of your surface material over the base gravel.

Tamp the base and surface gravel together using a plate compactor. Be careful not to disturb or damage the edging with the compactor.

Fill in the pathway with the remaining surface gravel. Drag a 2 × 4 across the tops of the edging using a sawing motion, to level the gravel flush with the edging.

Set the edging brick flush with the gravel using a mallet and 2 × 4.

Tamp the surface again using the plate compactor or a hand tamper. Compact the gravel so it is slightly below the top of the edging. This will help keep the gravel from migrating out of the path.

Rinse off the pathway with a hose to wash off dirt and dust and bring out the true colors of the materials.

Stepping stones blend beautifully into many types of landscaping, including rock gardens, ponds, flower or vegetable gardens, or even manicured lawns.

Pebbled Stepping Stone Path

A stepping stone path is both a practical and appealing way to traverse a landscape. With large stones as foot landings, you are free to use pretty much any type of fill material in between. You could even place stepping stones on individual footings over ponds and streams, making water the temporary infill that surrounds the stones. The infill does not need to follow a narrow path bed, either. Steppers can be used to cross a broad expanse of gravel, such as a Zen gravel patio or a smaller graveled opening in an alpine rock garden.

Stepping stones in a path serve two purposes: they lead the eye, and they carry the traveler. In both cases, the goal is rarely fast, direct transport, but more of a relaxing stroll that's comfortable, slow-paced, and above all, natural. Arrange the stepping stones in your walking path according to the gaits and strides of the people that are most likely to use the pathway. Keep in mind that our gaits tend to be longer on a utility path than in a rock garden.

Sometimes steppers are placed more for visual effect, with the knowledge that they will break the pacing rule with artful clusters of stones. Clustering is also an effective way to slow or congregate walkers near a fork in the path or at a good vantage point for a striking feature of the garden.

In the project featured here, landscape edging is used to contain the loose infill material (small aggregate), however a stepping stone path can also be effective without edging. For example, setting a series of steppers directly into your lawn and letting the lawn grass grow between them is a great choice as well.

TOOLS + MATERIALS

Mason's string	Coarse sand
Hose or rope	Thick steppers or broad river rocks with one flat face
Marking paint	
Sod stripper	¼ to ½" pond pebbles
Excavation tools	2½"-dia. river rock
Hand tamp	Eye protection
Wood stakes	Work gloves
1 × 2 lumber	Level
Straight 2 × 4	Rake
Edging	
Landscape fabric	

CHOOSING STEPPERS

Select beefy stones (minimum 2½ to 3½" thick) with at least one flat side. Thinner stepping stones tend to sink into the pebble infill. Stones that are described as stepping stones usually have two flat faces. For the desired visual effect on this project, we chose steppers and 12 to 24" wide fieldstones with one broad, flat face (the rounded face is buried in the ground, naturally).

Fieldstone with a flat face

Steppers

How to Make a Pebbled Stepping Stone Path

Excavate and prepare a bed for the path as you would for the gravel pathway (see pages 161 to 165), but use coarse building sand instead of compactable gravel for the base layer. Screed the sand flat so it's 2" below the top of the edging. Do not tamp the sand. *Tip: Low-profile plastic landscape edging is a good choice because it does not compete with the pathway.*

Moisten the sand bed, then position the stepping stones in the sand, spacing them for comfortable walking and the desired appearance. As you work, place a 2 × 4 across three adjacent stones to make sure they are even with one another. Add or remove sand beneath the steppers, as needed, to stabilize and level the stones.

Pour in a layer of larger infill stones (2"-dia. river rock is seen here). Smooth the stones with a garden rake. The infill should be below the tops of the stepping stones. Reserve about ⅓ of the larger diameter rocks.

Add the smaller infill stones that will migrate down and fill in around the larger infill rocks. To help settle the rocks, you can tamp lightly with a hand tamper, but don't get too aggressive—the larger rocks might fracture easily.

Scatter the remaining large infill stones across the infill area so they float on top of the other stones. Eventually, they will sink down lower in the pathway and you will need to lift and replace them selectively to maintain the original appearance.

Variations

A well-laid pebble path blends more seamlessly with a lush landscape or overgrown look. A more distinctively defined path in this backyard would have been out of place with the wild nature of the landscaping. As it is, this path helps create a sense of a secret shortcut.

Combine concrete stepping pavers with crushed rock or other small stones for a path with a cleaner, more contemporary look. Follow the same basic techniques used on pages 161 to 165, setting the pavers first, then filling in- between with the desired infill material(s).

Here we use gravel (small aggregate river rock), a common surface for paths and rock gardens, for the tread surfaces. Other tread surfaces include bricks, cobbles, and stepping stones. Even large flagstones can be fit to the tread openings.

Timber Garden Steps

Timberframed steps provide a delightfully simple and structurally satisfying way to manage slopes. They are usually designed with shallow steps that have long runs and large tread areas, that can be filled with a variety of materials. Two popular methods are shown here—gravel and poured concrete. Other tread surfaces you might consider are bricks, cobbles, and stepping stones. Even large flagstones can be cut to fit the tread openings.

Timber steps needn't follow the straight and narrow, either. You can vary the lengths of the left and right returns to create swooping helical steps that suggest spiral staircases. Or, increase the length of both returns to create a broad landing on which to set pots or accommodate a natural flattening of the slope. Want to soften the steps? Use soil as a base near the sides of the steps and plant herbs or ground cover. Or for a spring surprise, plant daffodils under a light pea gravel top dressing at the edges of the steps.

Timber steps don't require a frost footing, because the wooden joints flex with the earth rather than crack like solid concrete steps would. However, it's a good idea to include some underground anchoring to keep loose muddy soil from pushing the steps forward. To provide longterm stability, the gravel-filled steps shown here are secured to a timber cleat at the base of the slope, while concrete-filled steps are anchored at the base with long sections of pipe driven into the ground.

Designing steps is an important part of the process. Determine the total rise and run of the hill and translate this into a step size that conforms to this formula: 2× (rise) + run = 26 inches. Your step rise will equal your timber width, which can range from approximately 3½ inches (for 4 × 4 timbers or 4 × 6 on the flat) to 7¼ inches or 7½ inches (for 8 × 8 timbers). See page 141 for more help with designing and laying out landscape steps. As with any steps, be sure to keep the step size consistent so people don't trip.

How to Build Timber + Gravel Garden Steps

Install and level the timber cleat: mark the outline of the steps onto the ground using marking paint. Dig a trench for the cleat at the base of the steps. Add 2 to 4" of compactable gravel in the trench and compact it with a hand tamp. Cut the cleat to length and set it into the trench. Add or remove gravel beneath the cleat so it is level and its top is even with the surrounding ground or path surface.

Create trenches filled with tamped gravel for the returns (the timbers running back into the hill, perpendicular to the cleat and risers). The returns should be long enough to anchor the riser and returns of the step above. Dig trenches back into the hill for the returns and compact 2 to 4" of gravel into the trenches so each return will sit level on the cleat and gravel.

(continued)

Construction Details: Timber Step Frames

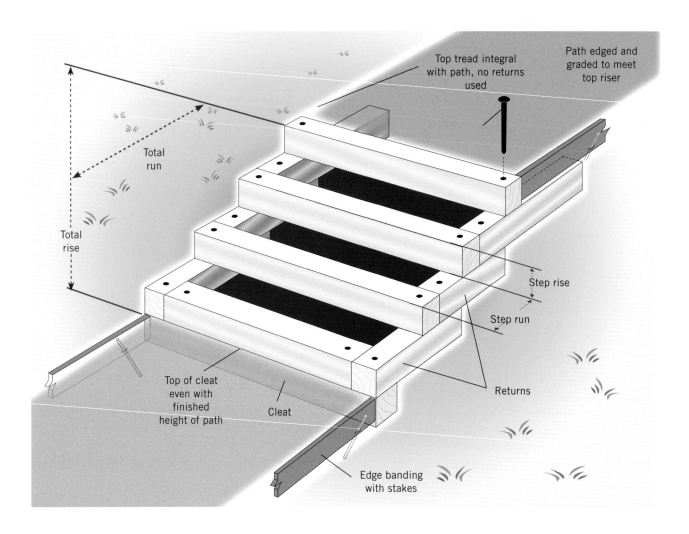

Total run

Total rise

Top of cleat even with finished height of path

Cleat

Top tread integral with path, no returns used

Path edged and graded to meet top riser

Step rise

Step run

Returns

Edge banding with stakes

 CUTTING TIMBERS

Large landscape timbers (6 × 6" and bigger) can be cut accurately and squarely with a circular saw, even though the saw's cutting capacity isn't big enough to do the job completely. First, draw cutting lines on all four sides of the timber using a speed square as guide. Next, cut along the line on all four sides with the saw set for maximum blade depth. Finally, use a hand saw to finish the cut. For most DIYers, this will yield a straighter cut than saws that can make the cut in one pass, such as a reciprocating saw.

Cut and position the returns and the first riser. Using a 2 × 4 as a level extender, check to see if the backs of the returns are level with each other and adjust by adding or removing gravel in the trenches. Drill four ⅜"-dia. holes and fasten the first riser and the two returns to the cleat with spikes.

Excavate and add tamped gravel for the second set of returns. Cut and position the second riser across the ends of the first returns, leaving the correct unit run between the riser faces. Note that only the first riser doesn't span the full width of the steps. Cut and position the returns, check for level, then predrill and spike the second riser and returns to the returns below.

Build the remaining steps in the same fashion. As you work, it may be necessary to alter the slope with additional excavating or backfilling (few natural hills follow a uniform slope). Add or remove soil as needed along the sides of the steps so that the returns are exposed roughly equally on both sides. Also, each tread should always be higher than the neighboring ground.

Install the final riser. Typically, the last timber does not have returns because its tread surface is integral with the path or surrounding ground. The top of this timber should be slightly higher than the ground. As an alternative, you can use returns to contain pathway material at the top of the steps.

(continued)

Lay and tamp a base of compactable gravel in each step tread area. Use a 2 × 4 as a tamper. For proper compaction, tamp the gravel in 2" or thinner layers before adding more. Leave about 2" of space in each tread for the surface material.

Fill up the tread areas with gravel or other appropriate material. Irregular crushed gravel offers maximum surface stability, while smooth stones, like the river rock seen here, blend into the environment more naturally and feel better underfoot than crushed gravel and stone.

Create or improve pathways at the top and bottom of the steps. For a nice effect, build a loose-fill walkway using the same type of gravel that you used for the steps. Install a railing, if desired or if required by the local building code.

Flagstone Garden Steps

Flagstone steps are perfect structures for managing natural slopes. Our design consists of broad flagstone treads and blocky ashlar risers, commonly sold as wall stone. The risers are prepared with compactable gravel beds on which the flagstone treads rest. For the project featured here, we purchased both the flagstone and the wall stone in their natural split state (as opposed to sawn). It may seem like overkill, but you should plan on purchasing 40 percent more flagstone, by square foot coverage, than your plans say you need. The process of fitting the stones together involves a lot of cutting and waste.

The average height of your risers is defined by the height of the wall stone available to you. These rough stones are separated and sold in a range of thicknesses (such as 3 to 4 inches), but hand-picking the stones helps bring them into a tighter range. The more uniform the thicknesses of your blocks, the less shimming and adjusting you'll have to do. (Remember, all of the steps must be the same size, to prevent a tripping hazard.) You will also need to stock up on slivers of rocks to use as shims to bring your risers and returns to a consistent height; breaking and cutting your stone generally produces plenty of these.

Flagstone steps work best when you create the broadest possible treads: think of them as a series of terraced patios. The goal, once you have the stock in hand, is to create a tread surface with as few stones as possible. This generally means you'll be doing quite a bit of cutting to get the irregular shapes to fit together. For a more formal look, cut the flagstones along straight lines so they fit together with small, regular gaps.

TOOLS + MATERIALS

Tape measure	Compactable gravel
Mason's string	Coarse sand
Marking paint	Wall stone
Line level	Flagstone
Torpedo level	Stone chisels
4-ft. level	Stone and block adhesive
Excavation tools	Rubber mallet
Maul	Eye protection
Hand tamp	Work gloves
Wood stakes	Small brush
Lumber (2 × 4, 4× 4)	Banker box (see page 86)
Straight 2 × 4	Spade
Landscape fabric	Granite or polymeric sand

Construction Details

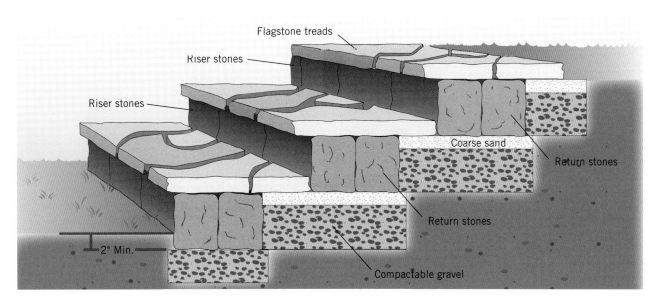

Flagstone treads
Riser stones
Riser stones
Coarse sand
Return stones
Return stones
2" Min.
Compactable gravel

How to Build Flagstone Garden Steps

Measure the height and length of the slope to calculate the rise and run dimensions for each step. Plot the footprint of your steps on the ground using marking paint. Purchase wall stones for your risers and returns in a height equal to the rise of your steps. Also buy flagstone (with approx. 40% overage) for the step treads.

Begin the excavation: for the area under the first riser and return stones, dig a trench to accommodate a 4" layer of gravel, plus the thickness of an average flagstone tread. For the area under the back edge of the first step's tread and the riser and return stones of the second step, dig to accommodate a 4" layer of gravel, plus a 1" layer of sand. Compact the soil with a 2 × 4 or 4 × 4.

Add a layer of compactable gravel to within 1" of the planned height and tamp. Add a top layer of compactable gravel and level it side to side and back to front. This top layer should be a flagstone's thickness below grade. This will keep the rise of the first step the same as the following steps. Leave the second layer of gravel uncompacted for easy adjustment of the riser and return stones.

Set the riser stones and one or two return stones onto the gravel base. Level the riser stones side to side by adding or removing gravel as needed. Level the risers front to back with a torpedo level. Allow for a slight up-slope for the returns (the steps should slope slightly downward from back to front so the treads will drain). Seat the stones firmly in the gravel with a hand maul, protecting the stone with a wood block.

Line the excavated area for the first tread with landscape fabric, draping it to cover the insides of the risers and returns. Add layers of compactable gravel and tamp down to within 1" of the tops of the risers and returns. Fill the remainder of the bed with sand and level it side to side with a 2 × 4. Slope it slightly from back to front. This layer of sand should be a little above the first risers and returns so that the tread stones will compact down to sit on the wall stones.

Set the second group of risers and returns: first, measure the step/run distance back from the face of your first risers and set up a level mason's string across the sand bed. Position the second-step risers and returns as you did for the first step, except these don't need to be dug in on the bottom because the bottom tread will reduce the risers' effective height.

Fold the fabric over the tops of the risers and trim off the excess. Set the flagstone treads of the first step like a puzzle, leaving a consistent distance between stones. Use large, heavy stones with relatively straight edges at the front of the step, overhanging the risers by about 2".

Fill in with smaller stones near the back. Cut and dress stones where necessary using stone chisels and a maul or mason's hammer (see pages 86 to 87 for tips on cutting stone). Finding a good arrangement takes some trial and error. Strive for fairly regular gaps, and avoid using small stones as they are easily displaced. Ideally, all stones should be at least as large as a dinner plate.

(continued)

Adjust the stones so the treads form a flat surface. Use a level as a guide, and add wet sand under thinner stones or remove sand from beneath thicker stones until all the flags come close to touching the level and are stable.

Shim between treads and risers with thin shards of stone. (Do not use sand to shim here). Glue the shards in place with block and stone adhesive. Check each step to make sure there is no path for sand to wash out from beneath the treads. You can settle smaller stones in sand with a mallet, but cushion your blows with a piece of wood.

Complete the second step in the same manner as the first. The bottoms of the risers should be at the same height as the bottoms of the tread on the step below. Continue building steps to the top of the slope. *Note: The top step often will not require returns.*

Fill the joints between stones with sand by sweeping the sand across the treads. Use coarse, dark sand such as granite sand, or choose polymeric sand, which resists washout better than regular builder's sand. Inspect the steps regularly for the first few weeks and make adjustments to the heights of stones as needed.

Pave the slope. Sometimes the best solution for garden steps is simply to lay some broad, flat rocks down on a pathway more or less as you find it. Make some effort to ensure that the surface of each rock is relatively flat and safe to walk on. Do not use this approach on steep slopes (greater than 2 in 12) or in heavily traveled areas.

These terraces are made from large flagstone steppers supported by stacked riser stones. They function as steps in managing the slope, but they look and feel more like a split-level patio. For a natural look and the best visual effect, terrace-type steps should mimic the topography of your yard.

Cut-limestone blocks that are roughly uniform in size are laid in a step formation to create a stately passageway up this small hill. A hand-formed mortar cap adorns the sides of the outdoor stairway for a more finished appearance.

Stacked slabs cannot be beat for pure simplicity, longevity, and ease of maintenance. The initial cost is high, and stacking stones that weigh several hundred pounds (or more) does require professionals with heavy equipment. But once these lovely garden steps are in place they'll stay put for generations with hardly any attention beyond a simple hosing off.

Low-Voltage Pathway + Patio Lighting

Patios are stages for relaxation, socializing, and pure enjoyment. That doesn't change after the sun goes down. Lighting your nighttime patio is a way to extend its usefulness and ensure safety, especially if the patio is some distance from the natural ambient light cast by the interior of the house.

The wonderful thing about landscape lighting around a patio or along a walkway is that the fixtures and type of light they cast can be decorative elements as well as serving a functional purpose.

When it comes to this type of lighting, low-voltage systems are by far the most popular. These systems use a step-down transformer to convert household 120-volt current to a safer 12-volt current that powers what are often LED lighting boards in each fixture (called "integrated fixtures"). These fixtures often don't have actual bulbs. That means no bulb to replace, but also means that when the light stops functioning, the entire fixture must be replaced (you can avoid this by purchasing "lamp-ready" fixtures).

The popularity is due to the ease of installation, the relative safety of the system (you're unlikely to ever experience an electrical shock from these systems, and if you do, it will be modest and benign), their modest expense, and the vast selection of fixture styles and finishes. These are also energy efficient, so they won't add much to your electric bill.

There are few limitations on low-voltage lighting placement. You'll need to dig a trench for the power cable that is at least 6 inches deep, and the transformer needs to be plugged into the nearest outdoor receptacle. Other than that, the fixtures can be placed anywhere the underfoot surface is soft enough for the post to go down into.

TOOLS + MATERIALS

Low-voltage lighting kit	Drill and bits
Tape measure	Screwdriver
Chalk, lime, or landscape spray paint	Wire stripper/cutter
Carpenter's pencil or grease pencil	Electrical tape
Garden spade, drain spade, or trenching shovel	Torpedo level

Thoughtfully placed and appropriately spaced low-voltage lighting fixtures not make the patio more attractive at night, they also serve as handy safety and security features.

Most landscapes and patios will benefit from a mix of lighting types. Here, uplight "spot lights" create dramatic silhouettes against the home's wall, while basic low-voltage fixtures add attractive ambient light that fills out the look.

Manufacturers offer different types of lighting fixtures in their low-voltage lighting kits. Choose the one that best serves your needs.

- **Spotlights.** These are usually directional and can often be adjusted to aim right at the feature you intend to highlight. Spotlights include downlights and uplights, which create a sense of visual drama. They are also often used to showcase particular features such as a waterfall or specimen planting. Spotlights are usually bulb-equipped fixtures. That allows you change the bulb for special effects, such as using colored bulbs for holiday displays.

- **Area lights.** This is the most common type of backyard lighting for decks, patios, stairs, and walkways; and it is the type used in this project. Area lighting projects soft, diffuse ambient illumination, usually down around the fixture and sometimes in all directions. It's a good general lighting, and there is an emphasis on the fixtures themselves as design elements.

- **Floodlights.** These are meant to provide maximum light on a specific area or feature, such as the wall of a house or over a significant part of a yard. Floodlights are most often associated with security (most home motion-sensor lights are floodlights). The fixtures themselves are rarely considered decorative or stylish elements. They usually meant to just blend into the surface on which they are mounted.

- **Well lights.** These are specialized fixtures meant to be partially or completely concealed in landscaping or structural elements such as flush-mount deck step lights. They become apparent only when lit, and are used where a subtle effect is desired. The light projected is limited and is used for safety and decorative purposes.

How to Install Low-Voltage Lighting

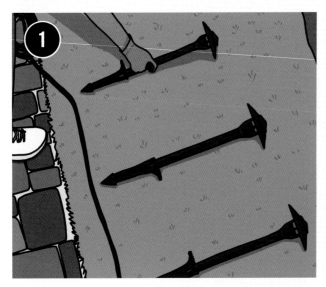

Check that all the pieces you'll need have been included in the kit, as listed on the box. Measure and physically lay out the lights and electrical cables in position, along the patio edge you'll be illuminating. Mark the locations of each light fixture with chalk, lime, or landscape spray paint.

Move the lights and cable out of the way, and dig the cable trench. The trench should be 6" deep. Use a garden spade if you have to cut into sod, or a drain spade or trenching shovel to dig the trench out of dirt.

Alternative: Some manufacturers—and some installers—recommend laying the cable on top of the soil and connecting the fixtures before burying the cable in the trench. You can also simply leave the cable on the ground if the walkway or patio edge is raised above ground level, or cover it with mulch or stone. However, burying the cable ensures it won't be disturbed.

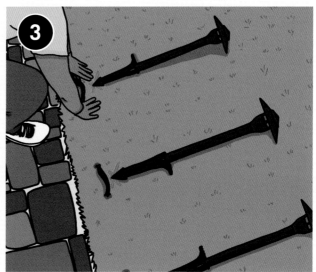

Carefully cover the cable with soil, but don't compact it. Leave a pinched half loop of cable pulled up and uncovered at each light fixture location. If you've removed sod, replace it, cutting an opening at each light location.

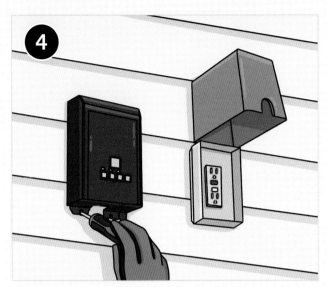

Position the transformer on the wall next to an exterior GFCI outlet and mark for the mounting screw holes. Drill holes at the marks and install anchors, if mounting on a masonry wall. Otherwise, screw the transformer in place using the supplied screws. *Note: Transformers must be mounted exactly as specified by the manufacturer to avoid fire or electrical failure risk. This usually entails mounting it with 1' of clearance all around, and using a heat shield for units that produce a lot of heat and that will be mounted on flammable surfaces.*

Split the two sides of the cable end at the transformer box, and strip about 1" of insulation from the end of each wire. Screw or clamp the wire ends into the transformer terminals.

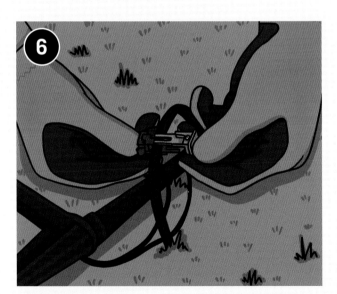

Connect each light fixture along the line by snapping the fixture's connectors onto the cable at the fixture location. Wrap the connection in electrical tape. Press the stake of the fixture support into the ground and check for level and plumb.

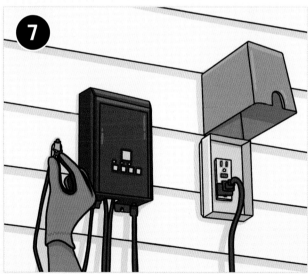

Plug in the transformer and check that all the lights work as intended. If the transformer includes a photo sensor, screw the bracket in place on the wall, secure the sensor end in the bracket, and plug the other end into the transformer. Otherwise, set the transformer timer.

Patio Rooms
+ Projects

A bare patio is like theater stage; it awaits the proper setting to really come to life. In the case of patios, however, there are significant functional concerns that inform any additions to the surface. Those can include wind, sun, and the prying eyes of neighbors. Any solution to which you turn in dealing with those issues is an opportunity to add beauty and style.

A perfect example is a shade sail. Although a simple patio umbrella may provide all the protection from direct midday sun that you need or want, most exposed patio rooms call for a bit more shade. Most homeowners are leery of adding a solid overhang—something that involves significant expense, a lot of time and effort, or both. Shade sails, like the project in this section, are a less expensive, more unique alternative. They not only shield a patio sitting area or outdoor bar or kitchen from sun, but also (to a limited degree) from summer showers. Not to mention, they can be a dramatic visual.

Of course, a full enclosure, including screens or windows, is a way to turn your summer patio into a three- or four-season outdoor room. Any enclosure involves careful consideration because even as you extend the patio's season, you may be diminishing it's sunbathing potential.

Other room additions, such as an outdoor kitchen or firepit, make a patio even more entertaining-friendly than it already is. A large fireplace can be converted into pizza oven, and a functional wet bar can be the centerpiece of a party patio.

In This Chapter:

- Underdeck Patio
- Runoff Gutters
- Patio Enclosure
- Screened Patio Room
- Patio Kitchen
- Shade Sails

Underdeck Patio

Second-story walk-out decks can be a mixed blessing. On top, you have an open, sun-filled perch with a commanding view of the landscape. The space below the deck, however, is all too often a dark and chilly nook unprotected from water runoff. As a result, an underdeck area often ends up as wasted space or becomes a holding area for seasonal storage items or the less desirable outdoor furniture.

But there's an easy way to reclaim all that convenient outdoor space—by installing a weatherizing ceiling system that captures runoff water from the deck above, leaving the area below dry enough to convert into a versatile outdoor room. You can even enclose the space to create a screened-in patio room.

The underdeck system featured in this project is designed for do-it-yourself installation. Its components are made to fit almost any standard deck and come in three sizes to accommodate different deck-joist spacing (for 12-inch, 16-inch, and 24-inch on-center spacing). Once the system is in place, the underdeck area is effectively "dried in," and you can begin adding amenities like overhead lighting, ceiling fans, and speakers to complete the outdoor room environment.

The system works by capturing water that falls through the decking above and channeling it to the outside edge of the deck. Depending on your plans, you can let the water fall from the ceiling panels along the deck's edge, or you can install a standard rain gutter and downspout to direct the water to a single exit point on the ground.

TOOLS + MATERIALS

4-ft. level	1" stainless steel screws
Chalk line	Rain gutter system (optional)
Drill	
Aviation snips	Eye protection
Hacksaw (for optional rain gutter)	Work gloves
	Tape measure
Underdeck ceiling system	Carpenter's pencil
Waterproof acrylic caulk (and caulk gun)	Color-matched caulk

Made of weather-resistant vinyl, this underdeck system creates an attractive, maintenance-free ceiling—the perfect shelter for an open-air or enclosed patio space below.

Design Tips

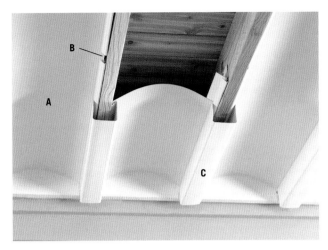

This underdeck system (see Resources, page 237) consists of four main parts: the joist rails mount to the deck joists and help secure the other components. The collector panels (A) span the joist cavity to capture water falling through the deck above. Water flows to the sides of the panels where it falls through gaps in the joist rails (B) and into the joist gutters (C) (for interior joists) and boundary gutters (for outer joists). The gutters carry the water to the outside edge of the deck.

For a finished look, paint the decking lumber that will be exposed after the system is installed. Typically, the lower portion of the ledger board (attached to the house) and the outer rim joist (at the outer edge of the deck) remain exposed.

Consider surrounding architectural elements when you select a system for sealing off the area below your deck. Here, the underdeck system is integrated with the deck and deck stairs both visually and functionally.

Check the undersides of several deck joists to make sure the structure is level. This is important for establishing the proper slope for effective water flow.

If your deck is not level, you must compensate for this when setting the ceiling slope. To determine the amount of correction that's needed, hold one end of the level against a joist and tilt the level until it reads perfectly level. Measure the distance from the joist to the free end of the level. Then, divide this measurement by the length of the level. For example, if the distance is ¼" and the level is 4 ft. long, the deck is out of level by ¹⁄₁₆" per foot.

To establish the slope for the ceiling system, mark the ends of the joists closest to the house. Measure up from the bottom 1" for every 10 ft. of joist length (or approximately ⅛" per ft.) and make a mark. Add or subtract the out-of-level factor from step 2.

Create each slope reference line using a chalk line. Hold one end of the chalk line at the mark made in Step 3, and hold the other end at the bottom edge of the joist where it meets the rim joist at the outside edge of the deck. Snap a reference line on all of the joists.

Install vinyl flashing along the ledger board in the joist cavities. Attach the flashing with 1" stainless steel screws. Caulk along the top edges of the flashing where it meets the ledger and both joists using quality, waterproof acrylic caulk. Also caulk the underside of the flashing for an extra layer of protection.

Begin installing the joist rails, starting 1" away from the ledger. Position each rail with its bottom edge on the chalk line, and fasten it to the joist at both ends with 1" stainless steel screws; then add one or two screws in between. Avoid overdriving the screws and deforming the rail. Leaving a little room for movement is best.

Install the remaining rails on each joist face, leaving a 1½" (minimum) to 2" (maximum) gap between rails. Install rails along both sides of each interior joist and along the insides of each outside joist. Trim the final rail in each row as needed using aviation snips.

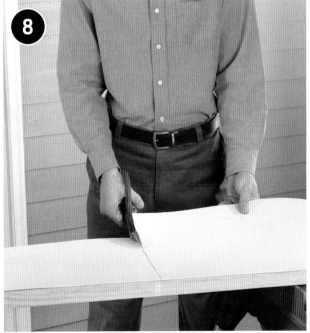

Measure the full length of each joist cavity, and cut a collector panel ¼" shorter than the cavity. This allows room for expansion of the panels. For narrower joist cavities, trim the panel to width following the manufacturer's sizing recommendations.

(continued)

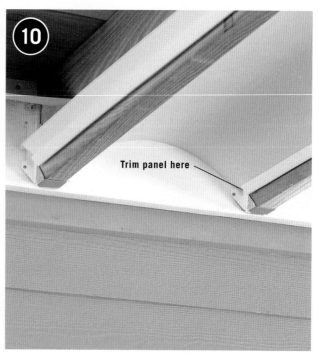

Scribe and trim the collector panels for a tight fit against the ledger board. Hold a carpenter's pencil flat against the ledger, and move the pencil along the board to transfer its contours to the panel. Trim the panel along the scribed line.

Trim the corners of the collector panels as needed to accommodate joist hangers and other hardware. This may be necessary only at the house side of the joist cavity; at the outer end, the ¼" expansion gap should clear any hardware.

Install the collector panels, starting at the house. With the textured side of the panel facing down, insert one side edge into the joist rails, and then push up gently on the opposite side until it fits into the opposing rails. When fully installed, the panels should be tight against the ledger and have a ¼" gap at the rim joist.

Prepare each joist gutter by cutting it ¼" shorter than the joist it will attach to. On the house end of each gutter, trim the corners of the flanges at 45°. This helps the gutter fit tightly to the ledger.

Cut four or five ⅛" tabs into the bottom surface at the outside ends of the gutters. This helps promote the drainage of water over the edge of the gutter.

Caulk here

Attach self-adhesive foam weatherstrip (available from the manufacturer) at the home-end of each joist gutter. Run a bead of caulk along the foam strip to water-seal it to the gutter. The weather strip serves as a water dam.

Install each joist gutter by spreading its sides open slightly while pushing the gutter up onto the joist rails until it snaps into place. The gutter should fit snugly against the collector panels. The gutter's home-end should be tight against the ledger with the ¼" expansion gap at the rim joist.

Prepare the boundary gutters following the same steps used for the joist gutters. Install each boundary gutter by slipping its long, outside flange behind the joist rails and pushing up until the gutter snaps into place. Install the boundary gutters working from the house side to the outer edge of the deck.

(continued)

Run a bead of color-matched caulk along the joint where the collector panels meet the ledger board. This is for decorative purposes only and is not required to prevent water intrusion.

If collector panels are misshapen because the joist spacing is too tight, free the panel within the problem area, then trim about ⅛" from the side edge of the panel. Reset the panel in the rails. If necessary, trim the panel edge again in slight increments until the panel fits properly.

WORKING AROUND BEAMS

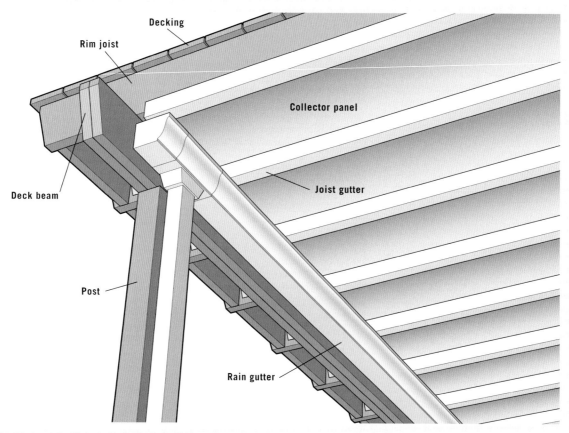

Decking

Rim joist

Collector panel

Deck beam

Joist gutter

Post

Rain gutter

For decks that have joists resting on top of a structural beam, stop the joist gutters and boundary gutters 1½" short of the beam. Install a standard rain gutter along the house-side of the beam to catch the water as it exits the system gutters. (On the opposite side of the beam, begin new runs of joist gutters that are tight against the beam and stop ¼" short of the rim joist. The joist rails and collector panels should clear the beam and can be installed as usual.) Or, you can simply leave the overhang area alone if you do not need water runoff protection below it.

Runoff Gutters

A basic gutter system for a square or rectangular deck includes a straight run of gutter channel with a downspout at one end. Prefabricated vinyl or aluminum gutter parts are ideal for this application. Gutter channels are commonly available in 10-foot and 20-foot lengths, so you might be able to use a single channel without seams. Otherwise, you can join sections of channel with special connectors. Shop around for the best type of hanger for your situation. If there's limited backing to support the back side of the channel or to fasten into, you may have to use strap-type hangers that can be secured to framing above the gutter.

Runoff gutters are installed at the ends of the underdeck channels to capture runoff water and redirect it away from the enclosed area through downspouts.

 ## How to Install an Underdeck Runoff Gutter

Snap a chalk line onto the beam or other supporting surface to establish the slope of the main gutter run. The line will correspond to the top edge of the gutter channel. The ideal slope is $\frac{1}{16}$" per foot. For example, with a 16-ft.-long gutter, the beginning is 1" higher than the end. The downspout should be located just inside the low end of the gutter channel. Mark the beam at both ends to create the desired slope, then snap a chalk line between the marks. The high end of the gutter should be just below the boundary gutter in the ceiling system.

(continued)

Install a downspout outlet near the end of the gutter run so the top of the gutter is flush with the slope line. If you plan to enclose the area under the deck, choose an inconspicuous location for the downspout, away from traffic areas.

Install hanger clips (depending on the type of hangers or support clips you use, it is often best to install them before installing the gutter channel). Attach a hanger every 24" so the top of the gutter will hang flush with the slope line.

TIP

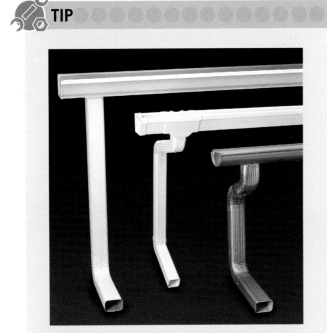

Gutters come in several material types, including PVC, enameled steel, and copper. In most cases you should try to match the surrounding trim materials, but using a more decorative material for contrast can be visually effective.

Cut sections of gutter channel to size using a hacksaw. Attach an end cap to the beginning of the main run, then fit the channel into the downspout outlet (allowing for expansion, if necessary) and secure the gutter in place.

5

Join sections of channel together, if necessary, for long runs using connectors. Install a short section of channel with an end cap on the opposite side of the downspout outlet. Paint the area where the downspout will be installed if it is unpainted.

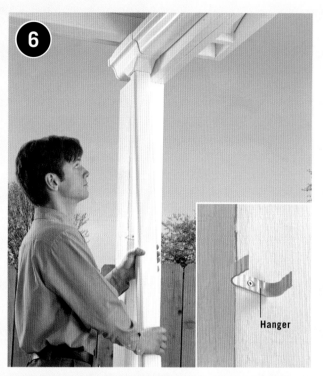

6

Hanger

Cut the downspout piping to length and fasten an elbow fitting to its bottom end. Attach the downspout to the downspout outlet, then secure the downspout to a post or other vertical support using hangers (inset).

7

Cut a drainpipe to run from the downspout elbow to a convenient drainage point. Position the pipe so it directs water away from the house and any traffic areas. Attach the pipe to the downspout elbow. Add a splash block, if desired.

ROUTING DRAINPIPES

You may have to get a little creative when routing the downspout drain in an enclosed porch or patio. Shown here, two elbows allow for a 90° turn of the drainpipe.

Patio Enclosure

If you like the openness and plentiful light of a patio but want more protection from rain and strong winds, this stylish, contemporary patio shelter may be just what you're looking for. Designed as a cross between an open-air arbor or pergola and an enclosed three-season porch, this patio structure has clear glazing panels on its roof and sides, allowing plenty of sunlight through while buffering the elements and even blocking harmful UV rays.

The roof of the patio shelter is framed with closely spaced 2 × 4 rafters to create the same light-filtering effects of a slatted arbor roof. The rafters are supported by a doubled-up 2 × 10 beam and 4 × 6 timber posts. Because the shelter is attached to the house, the posts are set on top of concrete foundation piers, or footings, that extend below the frost line. This prevents any shifting of the structure in areas where the ground freezes in winter.

The patio shelter's side panels cut down on wind while providing a degree of privacy screening. Their simple construction means you can easily alter the dimensions or locations of the panels to suit your own plans. In the project shown, each side has two glazing panels with a 3½-inch space in between, for airflow. If desired, you can use a single sheet of glazing across the entire side section. The glazing is held in place with wood strips and screws so they can be removed for seasonal cleaning.

Slats of white oak sandwich clear polycarbonate panels to create walls that block the wind without blocking light and views.

Building against a solid wall and not in front of a patio door makes the space inside this contemporary shelter much more usable. The corrugated roof panels (see Resources, page 237) made of clear polycarbonate allow light to enter while keeping the elements out.

PATIO ENCLOSURE PLANS

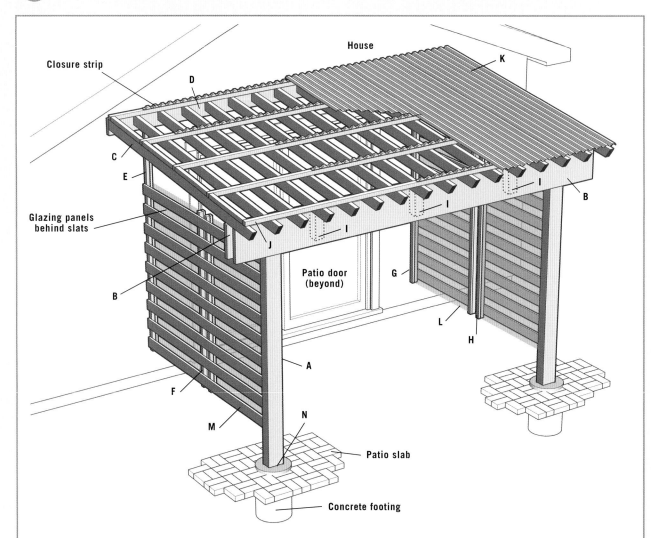

Labels in the illustration:
House
Closure strip
K
D
C
E
Glazing panels behind slats
B
I
I
I
B
J
Patio door (beyond)
G
L
H
A
F
M
N
Patio slab
Concrete footing

Plan your own patio shelter based on the requirements set by the local building code. Your city's building department or a qualified building professional can help you with the critical structural specifications, such as the size and depth of the concrete post footings, the sizing of beam members, and the overall roof construction. The building department will help make sure your shelter is suitable for the local weather conditions (particularly wind and snow loads).

CUTTING LIST

KEY	PART	NO.	SIZE	MATERIAL	KEY	PART	NO.	SIZE	MATERIAL
A	Post	2	3½ × 5½ × 144"	4 × 6 treated pine	H	Slat cleat cap	4	¾ × 1½ × 60"	1 × 2 pine
B	Beam member	2	1½ × 9¼ × 120"*	2 × 10 treated pine	I	Beam blocks	3	3½ × 3½ × 8"	4 × 4 pine
C	Rafter	16	1½ × 3½ × 120"*	2 × 4 pine	J	Purlin	5	1½ × 1½ × 120"	2 × 2 pine
D	Ledger	1	1½ × 5½ × 144"	2 × 6 treated pine	K	Roof panel	6	¼ × 26 × 96"	Corrugated polycarbonate
E	Back post	2	1½ × 1½ × 96"*	2 × 2 pine	L	Side panel	4	¼ × 36 × 58"	Clear polycarbonate
F	Slat cleat	4	1½ × 1½ × 60"	2 × 2 pine	M	Slat	18	¾ × 3½ × 80"*	White oak
G	Back post cap	2	¾ × 1½ × 96"*	1 × 2 pine	N	Post base	2	1½ × 3½ × 3½"	

*Size listed is prior to final trimming

TOOLS + MATERIALS

Chalk line
4-ft. level
Plumb bob
Mason's string
Digging tools
Concrete mixing tools
Circular saw
Ratchet wrench
Line level
Reciprocating saw or handsaw
Drill with bits
Finish application tools
Gravel
12"-dia. concrete tube forms
Concrete mix
⅝"-dia. J-bolts

⅜ × 4" corrosion resistant lag screws
Flashing
Silicone caulk
Corrosion-resistant metal post bases and hardware
Lumber
Corrosion-resistant 16d and 8d common nails
½"-dia. corrosion-resistant lag bolts and washers
Exterior wood glue or construction adhesive
Corrosion-resistant framing anchors (for rafters)
Deck screws (1½, 3")
Polycarbonate roofing panels

Clear polycarbonate panels
Closure strips
Roofing screws with EPDM washers
Roofing adhesive/sealant
Wood finishing materials
Neoprene weatherstripping
Scrap lumber
Exterior wood stain
Stakes
Eye protection
Hammer
Caulk gun
Table saw, router, or circular saw
Work gloves

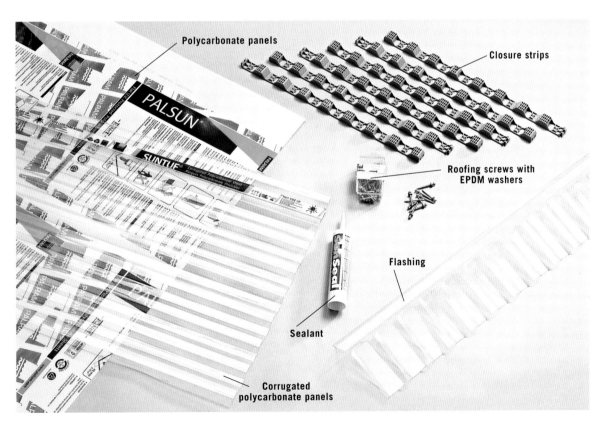

Polycarbonate panels

Closure strips

Roofing screws with EPDM washers

Flashing

Sealant

Corrugated polycarbonate panels

The roofing and side glazing panels of the patio shelter are made with tough polycarbonate materials. The corrugated roofing panels allow up to 90% light transmission while blocking virtually 100 percent of harmful UV rays. The flat side panels offer the transparency of glass but are lighter and much stronger than glass. Also shown is: wall flashing designed to be tucked under siding; closure strips that fit between the 2 × 2 purlins and the corrugated roof panels; self-sealing screws and polycarbonate sealant.

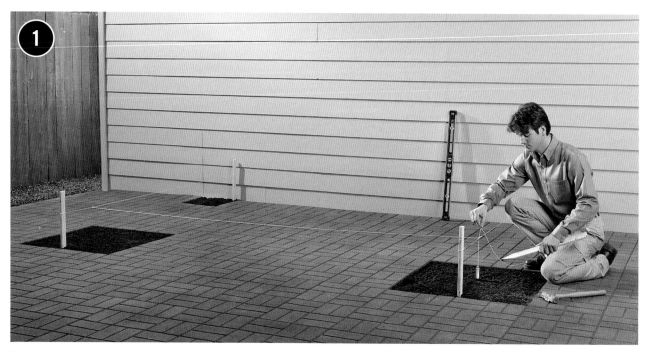

Mark the layout for the ledger board on the house wall. Lay out the post footing locations in the patio area. To mark the cutout for the ledger board, include the width of the ledger board, plus the height of the roofing, plus 1½" for the flashing. The length of the cutout should be 1" longer than the length of the ledger board (12 ft. as shown). Plumb down from the ends of the ledger, then measure in to mark the locations of the post centers. At each of these points, run a perpendicular string line from the house out to about 2 ft. beyond the post locations. Set up a third string line, perpendicular to the first two, to mark the centers of the posts. Plumb down from the string line intersections and mark the post centers on the ground with stakes.

Dig a hole for a concrete tube form at each post location following the local building code for the footing depth. Add 6" of gravel and tamp it down. Position the tube forms so they are plumb and extend at least 2" above the ground. Backfill around them with soil and compact thoroughly.

Fill the tube forms with concrete and screed it level with the tops of the forms. At each post-center location, embed a J-bolt into the wet concrete so it extends the recommended distance above the top of the form. Let the concrete cure.

Cut out the house siding for the ledger board using a circular saw. Cut only through the siding, leaving the wall sheathing. *Note: If the sheathing is fiberboard instead of plywood, you may have to remove the fiberboard; consult your local building department.* Replace any damaged building paper covering the sheathing.

Stain the wood parts before you begin installing the shelter closure strips and panels. We used a black, semitransparent deck and siding stain.

Apply a protective finish to the wood slats as desired. We used a semitransparent deck stain.

(continued)

Install the ledger. First, slip corrugated roof flashing or metal roof flashing behind the siding above the ledger cutout so the vertical flange extends at least 3" above the bottom of the siding. Cut the ledger board to length. Fasten the ledger to the wall using ⅜ × 4" lag screws driven through counterbored pilot holes at each wall-stud location. Seal over the screw heads and counterbores with silicone caulk.

Anchor the post bases to the concrete footing, securing them with the base manufacturer's recommended hardware. Make sure the bases are aligned with each other and are perpendicular to the house wall.

Cut off the bottom ends of the posts so they are perfectly square. Set each post in its base and hold it plumb. Fasten the post to the base using the manufacturer's recommended fasteners. Brace the posts with temporary bracing. *Note: You will cut the posts to length in a later step.*

Cut a pattern rafter from 2 × 4 lumber using the desired roof slope to find the angle cut for the top end. Angle the bottom end as desired for decorative effect. Set the rafter in position so its top end is even with the top of the ledger and its bottom end passes along the side of a post. Mark along the bottom edge of the rafter onto the post. Repeat to mark the other post. Use a string and line level to make sure the post marks are level with each other.

Cut the inner beam member to length from 2 × 10 lumber, then bevel the top edge to follow the roof slope. Position the board so its top edge is on the post markings, and it overhangs the posts equally at both ends (12" of overhang is shown). Tack the board in place with 16d nails.

Cut the outer beam member to length from 2 × 10 lumber. Bevel the top edge following the roof slope, and remove enough material so that the bottom edges of the two beam members will be level with each other. Tack the member in place with nails.

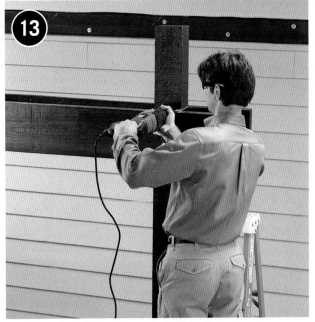

Anchor the beam members together and to the posts with pairs of ½"-dia. lag bolts and washers. Cut the posts off flush with the tops of the beam members using a handsaw or reciprocating saw.

(continued)

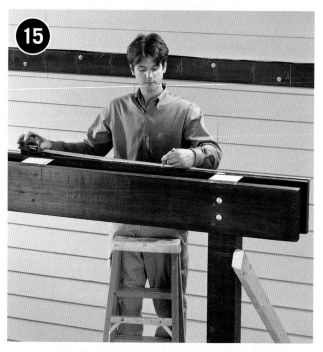

Trim the cutoff post pieces to length and use them as blocking between the beam members. Position the blocks evenly spaced between the posts and fasten them to both beam members with glue and 16d nails. *Note: Diagonal bracing between the posts and beam may be recommended or required in some areas; consult your local building department.*

Mark the rafter layout onto the ledger and beam. As shown here, the rafters are spaced 9½" apart on center. The two outer rafters should be flush with the ends of the ledger and beam.

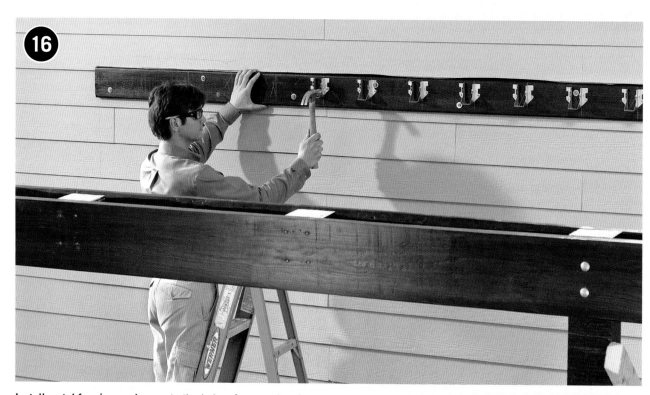

Install metal framing anchors onto the ledger for securing the top rafter ends using the anchor manufacturer's recommended fasteners. Use the pattern rafter or a block to position the anchors so the rafters will be flush with the top of the ledger.

17

Use the pattern rafter to mark the remaining rafters and then cut them. Install the rafters one at a time. Fasten the top ends to the metal anchor using the recommended fasteners. Fasten the bottom ends to both beam members by toenailing one 8d nail through each rafter side and into the beam member.

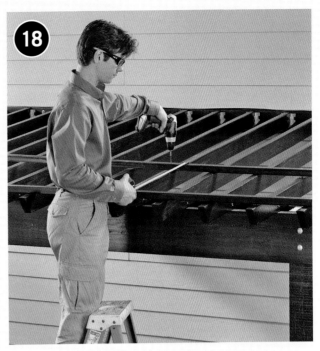

18

Install the 2 × 2 purlins perpendicular to the rafters using 3" deck screws. Position the first purlin a few inches from the bottom ends of the rafters. Space the remaining purlins 24" on center. The ends of the purlins should be flush with the outside faces of the outer rafters.

19

Add 2 × 2 blocking between the purlins along the outer rafters, and fasten them with 3" deck screws. This blocking will support the vertical closure strips for the roof panels.

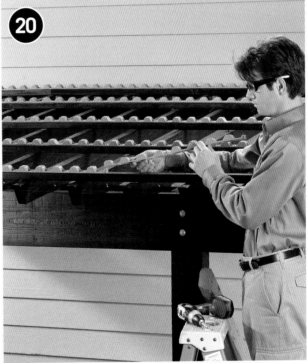

20

Starting at one side of the roof, install the roof panel closure strips over the purlins using the manufacturer's recommended fasteners. Begin every run of strips from the same side of the roof, so the ridges in the strips will be aligned.

(continued)

Add vertical closure strips over the 2 × 2 purlin blocking to fill in between the horizontal strips.

Position the first roofing panel along one side edge of the roof. The inside edge of the panel should fall over a rafter. If necessary, trim the panel to length or width following the manufacturer's recommendations.

Drill pilot holes, and fasten the first panel to the closure strips with the recommended type of screw and rubber washer. Fasten the panel at the peak (top) of every other corrugation. Drive the screws down carefully, stopping when the washer contacts the panel but is not compressed. This allows for thermal expansion of the panel.

Apply a bead of the recommended adhesive/sealant (usually supplied by the panel manufacturer) along the last trough of the roofing panel. Set the second panel into place, overlapping the last troughs on both panels. Fasten the second panel. Install the remaining panels using the same procedure. Caulk the seam between the roof panels and the roof flashing.

25

Blade guard removed for clarity

To create channels for the side glazing panels, mill a rabbet into each of the eight vertical 2 × 2 cleats. Consult the glazing manufacturer for the recommended channel size, making sure to provide space for thermal expansion of the panels. Mill the rabbets using a table saw, router, or circular saw. Stop the rabbets so the bottom edges of the panels will be even with, or slightly above, the bottom edge of the lowest side slat.

 TIP

If you do not have wall flashing designed to work with the roof profile, place closure strips upside down onto the roof panels and run another bead of adhesive/sealant over the tops of the strips. Work the flashing down and embed it into the sealant. Seal along all exposed edges of the ledger with silicone caulk.

26

Position a cleat on each post at the desired height, with the cleat centered from side to side on the post. The rabbeted corner should face inside the shelter. Fasten the cleats to the posts with 3" deck screws. Fasten two more cleats to the house wall so they are aligned and level with the post cleats.

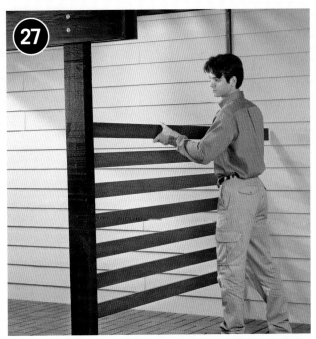

27

Cut the side slats to length to fit between the posts and the house wall. Mark the slat layouts onto the outside faces of the cleats, and install the slats with 1½" deck screws or exterior trim-head screws. Space the slats 3½" apart or as desired.

(continued)

28

Fasten the middle cleats to the slats on each side, leaving about 3½" of space between the cleats (or as desired). The cleats should overhang the top and bottom slats by 1½" (or as desired).

TIP

Used for decorative accent slats on this patio shelter, white oak is a traditional exterior wood that was employed for boatbuilding as well as outdoor furnishings. Although it requires no finishing, we coated the white oak with a dark, penetrating wood stain to bring out the grain.

29

Cut the cap strips for the glazing panels from 1 × 2 material (or rip down strips from the 1 × 4 slat material). Position each cap over a cleat and drill evenly spaced pilot holes through the cap and into the cleat. Make sure the holes go into the solid (non-rabbeted) portion of the cleat. Drill counterbores, too (left). Drive screws to attach the post caps (right).

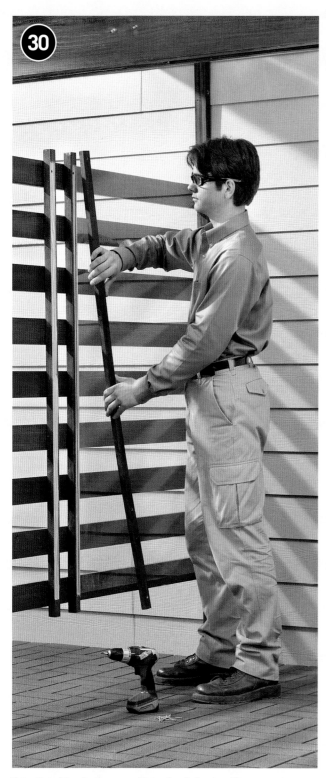

Trim the side glazing panels to size following the manufacturer's directions. Apply neoprene or EPDM stripping or packing to the side edges of the panels. Fit each panel into its cleat frame, cover the glazing edges with the 1 × 2 caps, and secure the caps with 1½" deck screws. *Note: If the glazing comes with a protective film, remove the film during this step as appropriate and make sure the panel is oriented for full UV protection.*

Option: Add a 2 × 4 decorative cap on the outside face of each post. Center the cap side-to-side on the post and fasten it with 16d casing nails.

Screened Patio Room

A screening system is an ingeniously simple and effective way to enclose a covered patio—leaving you free to enjoy the outdoors at any time of day without the annoyance of insects and other pests. A basic system includes three main components: a base channel that mounts directly to the patio-roof posts, railings, and other framing members (as applicable); the screening (and spline); and a trim cap that snaps in place over the base channel to cover the screen edges and add a finished look to the installation. The base cap pieces are made to go together, but the screen and spline may need to be purchased separately. Be sure to follow the system manufacturer's specifications for screen type and spline size. Screen systems are typically compatible with standard fiberglass and aluminum screen materials.

With the system shown in this project, each piece of screen is secured into the base channels using standard vinyl or rubber spline and a spline roller. The screen goes up quickly and easily after a little practice, and it doesn't have to be perfectly tight right away; when the cap pieces are snapped on, they add tension to the screening, pulling it tight from all sides of the opening. This does a good job of eliminating the unsightly sag that occurs all too quickly with standard stapled-up screening. Replacing screen sections also is much easier with a screen system: just remove the surrounding cap pieces, pull out the spline, and install a new piece of screen.

TOOLS + MATERIALS

Pruning sheers or aviation snips

Drill with bits

Spline roller

Utility knife

Rubber mallet

Screen system components

Level

Corrosion-resistant deck screws (1, 3½")

Screening

Spline cord

2×4 lumber or composite equivalent

Straightedge

Power hand planer

Exterior construction adhesive (and caulk gun)

Concrete anchors or deck screws

Eye protection

Clamps

Circular saw

Work gloves

Carpenter's square

Tape measure

Wood shims

Hinges and fasteners

Galvanized finish nails

Screen door handles, latches, and closer hardware

Screen systems are quick, easy products for screening in covered patios, including underdeck spaces like the patio shown here.

With their textures and grain, plain wood posts are fine for most homes. But when you combine them with gleaming new white vinyl-based products, they can look a little rough. One way to make your patio-roof posts blend better when you're installing underdeck or screening systems is to clad them and paint them to match. Traditionally, clear dimensional lumber is used for the cladding. But to get seamless results, this often means you need to cut complicated dado-rabbet joints that run all the way from top to bottom at each corner. Then, you need to sand thoroughly and apply several coats of paint. An easier option for making all of your screen system parts match is to clad posts with one-piece PVC post cladding (see Resources, page 237). The product shown here is designed to fit around a 6 × 6" post. On the interior surface it is kerfed but the exterior vinyl surface is solid. This way, it can be bent around corners crisply and seamlessly.

Spline-based screening systems are available at home centers and hardware stores and through many websites. Screen Tight, the system shown here (see Resources, page 237), is made with UV-resistant PVC and is available with trim colors of white, gray, beige, and brown. Parts of the system include: stretchable spline cord (A); spline roller (B); adhesive for bonding rigid vinyl (C); storm door handles (D); storm door hinges (E); 1" corrosion-resistant screws (F); screw-eye door latch (G); deck screws (H); decorative cap screws (I); track cap (J); track base (K); composite 2 × 4 (L); fiberglass screening (M).

How to Install a Screening System

Begin installing the track backers that frame the openings you will be screening. You may use pressure-treated 2 × 4s or 2 × 2s. For a long-lasting and low-maintenance framework, we used composite 2 × 4–sized backers that came with the screen system materials. These products are not rated for structural use. Attach the backers to the inside faces of the posts, centered, using exterior construction adhesive and 3½" deck screws.

Secure sole plates to the patio using construction adhesive and appropriate fasteners (use concrete anchors for concrete, stone, or paver patios and use deck screws for wood and nonwood patios).

Attach cap plates to the beam or joist at the top of the installation area, leaving 1½" between plates to create recesses for the vertical backers.

Install the vertical track backer members with the top ends fitted in the gaps you left in the cap plate. Make sure the vertical members are plumb and then drive deck screws toenail style through the members and into the sole plate. Also drive screws up at angles through the vertical members and into the beam or joist at the top of the area. Drill pilot holes.

Install the door header and the horizontal track backers using adhesive and deck screws. Locate the horizontal members 36 to 42" above the ground.

Cut a base channel to length for each vertical member in the screen frame. At the tops of the posts, hold the base channel back to allow room for the horizontal channels, if applicable). This results in less cutting of the cap trim later. Cut the channels using pruning shears or aviation snips.

Fasten the vertical channel pieces to the framing with 1" corrosion-resistant screws. Drive a screw into each predrilled hole in the channel, then add a screw 2" from each end. Drive each screw in snugly but not so far that it warps the channel.

Cut the horizontal base channels to length and install them with screws. The butted joints where the horizontal channels meet the verticals don't have to be precise or tight-fitting.

(continued)

Begin installing the screen by positioning a full piece of screening over an opening so it overlaps several inches on all sides. Secure the screen into the horizontal base channel at one of the top corners using spline cord. You can run the spline around the corners or cut it off at the ends as needed.

Embed the spline at the starting point, where it should fit fully into the groove of the base channel. Use a spline roller. Then, using one hand to pull the screen taut, press the spline into place to secure the screen along the top of the opening.

Secure the screen along both sides, then along the bottom using the same technique as for the top. When you're finished, the screen should be flat and reasonably tight, with no sagging or wrinkling. If you make a mistake or the screen won't cooperate, simply remove the spline and start over.

Trim off the excess screening with a sharp utility knife. Fiberglass screen cuts very easily, so control the knife carefully at all times. Repeat steps as needed to screen in the remaining openings.

Install the trim caps over the base channels, starting with the vertical pieces. Working from the bottom up, center the cap over the base, then tap it into place using a rubber mallet. *Tip: If you have a continuous horizontal band along the top of the screening, install those trim pieces before capping the verticals.*

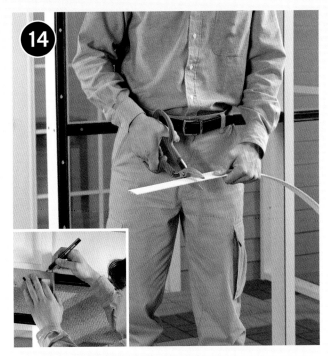

Cut the cap pieces to length as you install them. Mark cutting lines with a pencil, and make the cuts with pruning shears or aviation snips. If desired, use a square to mark a straight cutting line across the face or backside of the trim cap (inset).

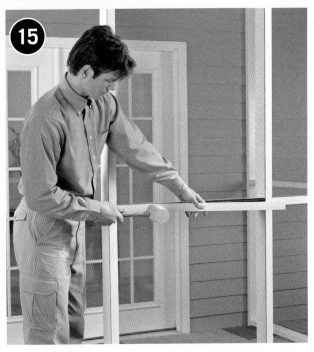

Install the horizontal pieces once the vertical cap pieces are in place using the same techniques. Butt the horizontals tight against the verticals to start each piece, and then trim it to length as you approach the opposite end.

Complete the screening project by installing a screen door. A low-maintenance vinyl door provides a good match with the finish of the vinyl trim cap, but a traditional painted wood door is also appropriate.

Option: To protect the screening from being damaged by pets, kids, or other causes, make lattice frames and install them in the framed areas.

How to Install a Screen Door

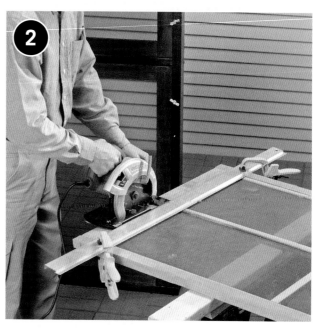

Measure the door opening. The new screen door should be ¼ to ⅜" narrower and ¼ to ½" shorter than the opening. Plan to trim the door, if necessary, for proper clearance. Some vinyl doors should not be cut, while others may be cut only a limited amount. If the door is vinyl, check with the manufacturer.

To trim the height of a door, mark the cutting line, then clamp a straightedge to the door to guide your circular saw for a straight cut. For wood doors, score deeply along the cutting line with a utility knife before setting up the straightedge; this prevents splintering on the top side when cutting across the grain.

To trim the width of a wood door, it's usually best to remove material from the hinge side, which is less visible. Mark a full-length cutting line, and make the cut with a circular saw. Or, you can use a power hand planer to trim off material from the edge (shown in photo). Use sand paper or a file to round-over the cut side (and bottom, if applicable) edges to match the uncut edges and to prevent splinters.

Test-fit the door in the opening using wood shims along the bottom to raise the door to the right height. Center the door from side to side; the reveal here should be about ⅛" on each side.

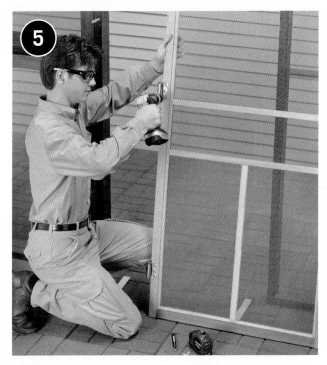

Install surface-mount hinges to the door using screws driven into pilot holes (three hinges is preferable, but two will work for most doors). Position the top hinge about 7" from the top of the door, the bottom hinge about 10" from the bottom, and the middle hinge halfway between the other two.

Hang the door. Set the door into the opening using shims at the sides to establish equal reveals. Mark and drill pilot holes for the hinges, then screw the hinges to the side jamb or post to hang the door.

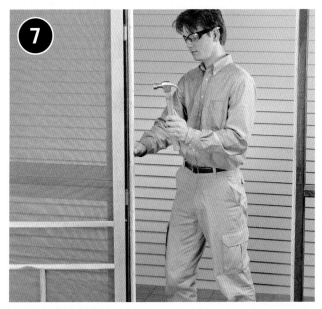

Install doorstop molding around the sides and top of the door opening using galvanized finish nails if your screen door is not prehung. Position the stops so the outer door face is flush with the outer jamb edges, trim, or door posts, as applicable. Install the stop along the top of the opening first, then along the sides.

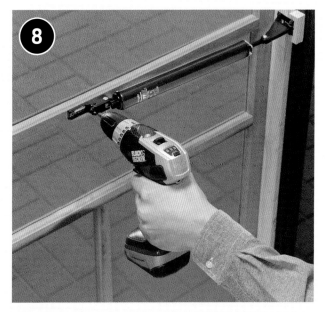

Add door handles, latches, and closer hardware as desired, following the manufacturer's instructions. A closer is a good idea to prevent the door from being left open and admitting insects. Closers come in a range of types, including spring-loaded hinges, hydraulic pistons, and old-fashioned extension springs. Most also have a stop chain that prevents the door from blowing all the way open.

Patio Shade Sails

Sun exposure can be unpredictable. Homeowners often discover that the patio they laid in spring when the area enjoyed dappled shade, becomes an uncomfortable heat sink by mid-summer.

You can't move the patio, but you can get relief with a shade sail. These are made of special fabrics that effectively block direct sunlight and UV rays. They can also provide an interesting and eye-catching addition to most outdoor areas.

Sails are mounted under tension, which means they have to be attached to stable, secure surfaces that will support the sail even under wind load. Many are mounted to posts, but sails covering patios attached, or close to the house, are secured to a wall. The attachment point must be fastened to underlying framing for proper security. Where post mounting, manufacturers generally specify a minimum 6 × 6 wood, or 4 to 5 inch steel post. Screw eyes are usually used with wood and through-bolts with steel.

The sails are attached at corners, using a D shackle linked into an adjustable turnbuckle or tensioner. That, in turn, is fastened to the threaded hook eye or eye bolt. Properly tensioning the sail with the turnbuckle or tensioner is key to avoiding wrinkles in the sail and ensuring long term safety.

In some cases, the manufacturer may allow the use of a cable or chain to bridge the distance between the shade-sail eyelet and the support. This is useful when, for example, the shade sail will stop halfway across an already laid patio. The posts will need to be driven at the edge of the patio, far from the corners of the sail.

The sail in this project is a modest three-sided sail. As with any shade sail installation, the sail here is sloped in one direction to allow it drain efficiently, and shed leaves or snow. Although the fabric is somewhat permeable, shade sails are not porous.

If you're installing a larger sail, it's a good idea to get engineering input from either the seller or an independent structural engineer. Special posts are often sold with larger sails, and specialized versions—such as those that can be fastened to a deck edge—are offered. You can also custom order posts for specific applications. Regardless, look for signs of quality in any shade sail you're considering. Those include stainless steel hardware and wide, double-stitched seams.

TOOLS + MATERIALS

Tape measure	Concrete
Sharpie	Drill and bits
Shade sail and hardware	White lithium grease
(3) 4 × 4" × 10' pressure-treated or cedar shade sail support posts	Crescent wrench
	Come-along tool (optional)
Landscape spray paint	Work gloves
Auger (optional)	Safety glasses
Post hole digger	Quick-set concrete mix
Shovel	Concrete float

How to Install a Shade Sail

Note sun exposure in the area and measure and mark the placement and positioning of the sail accordingly (consult the manufacturer's recommendations for guidance). Lay the sail in position to double check the distance between the mounting attachment points. Mark post positions with landscape spray paint and remove the sail. Double-check the outside distances between mount attachments on all sides before proceeding.

Dig the post holes for the support posts, to the depth and width recommended by the shade sail manufacturer. Fill each hole with 4" of gravel and stand the posts in the holes. Double-check the measurements between the mounting points on the posts.

Place the first post in the hole and fill with concrete around it. Ensure the post is plumb and then brace it until the concrete has set. Repeat with the other two posts. *Note: It's ideal to use a composite or plastic sleeve to protect the ends of wood posts and prevent rotting and subsequent post failure.*

(continued)

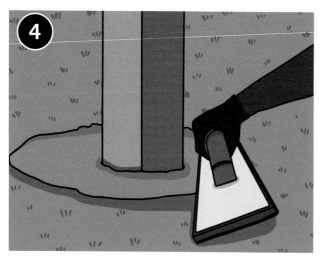

Smooth the top of the footing with a trowel or concrete float. If you are using steel posts, slip a post onto the anchor bolts and check post-to-post measurements again. Ensure plumb and tighten down the bolts. Repeat with the other two posts. *Note: Footings can be poured at the same time as a poured concrete patio, but the footings will need to be deeper. Follow footing size specifications supplied by the manufacturer.*

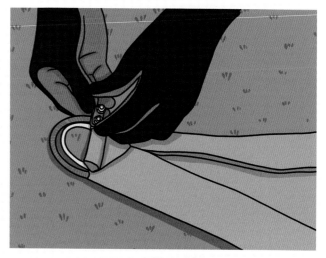

Optional: Lay the shade in position. Make sure it is oriented correctly. If your sail came with wire rope, run it through the hem pocket. The rope is normally run over the top of the attachment rings, with the ends looped back into the hem at the final corner. Clamp the rope at that corner, leaving the clamps loose.

Double-check the measurements from the ground up for the post attachments (remember: the attachment points should be at different heights to ensure proper drainage). Screw the pad eyes to the posts using the supplied screws.

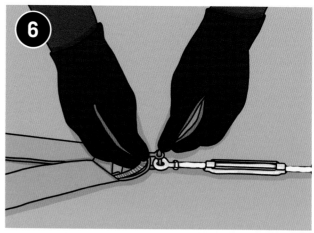

Extend the turnbuckle ends as far as they will open. Grease the threads with white lithium grease. Connect the shade sail eyelet to one end of a turnbuckle using a snap hook or U shackle (whichever came with your sail). Repeat for the other corners and then fasten the turnbuckles at each corner to the appropriate post pad eye.

Shade sails are mounted under tension to resist wind and water loads. In some cases, it may be a challenge to connect the final corner of a shade sail to its attachment point. Different manufacturers recommend different techniques for dealing with this situation. The simplest, least expensive option is to tie one end of a sturdy rope or paracord to the sail's D ring, and wind the other end through the pad eye, then back through both. Pull the rope until the two sides are close enough to attach the turnbuckle (below left, this may require a helper). The easier method is to use a mechanical come-along tool. Attach one end to the sail corner and one to the post attachment (below right) and ratchet the two sides close enough to attach the turnbuckle.

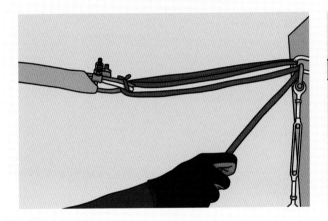

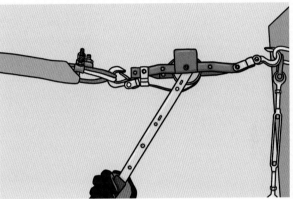

Return to the first corner you attached, and tighten the turnbuckle by turning the body with a crescent wrench. Continue tightening the turnbuckles all around until there are no wrinkles in the sail.

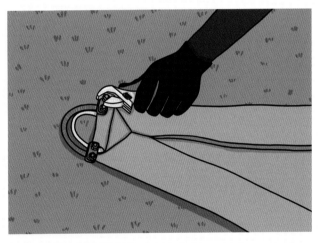

Optional: Finally, tighten the internal wire rope clamps for the hem pocket wire rope, if any, to hold the rope in place. (Many home shade sails do not include a wire rope.)

A Patio Kitchen

A simple summer barbecue is fun, but a full-fledged al fresco dinner from an outdoor kitchen is fun multiplied. Using stacked pavers is a simple, quick way to create a wonderful outdoor kitchen and a poured concrete countertop is just as easy and super durable.

The project outlined here provides instructions for a simple L-shaped kitchen base. One of the great things about this design is that the foot print is remarkably adaptable. Paver suppliers even offer diagrams and instructions for creating different patterns with the pavers. Use them to lay your own unique look.

Change up the concrete countertop mold to accommodate a gas cooktop, or any other feature. Using concrete means the surface is rugged enough to hold up to food prep and the weather over time much better than marble or granite would—with a fraction of the installation effort and cost.

TOOLS + MATERIALS

Pavers (three sizes)	Clean rubber tub
Tape measure	Quick-set countertop
Chalk line	concrete mix
Framing square	Polymer construction
Painter's tape	adhesive
6 mil plastic sheeting	Caulk gun
4" level	Safety glasses
6' clear 2 × 4	Work gloves
Concrete trowel	Latex gloves
Quick-set concrete mix	

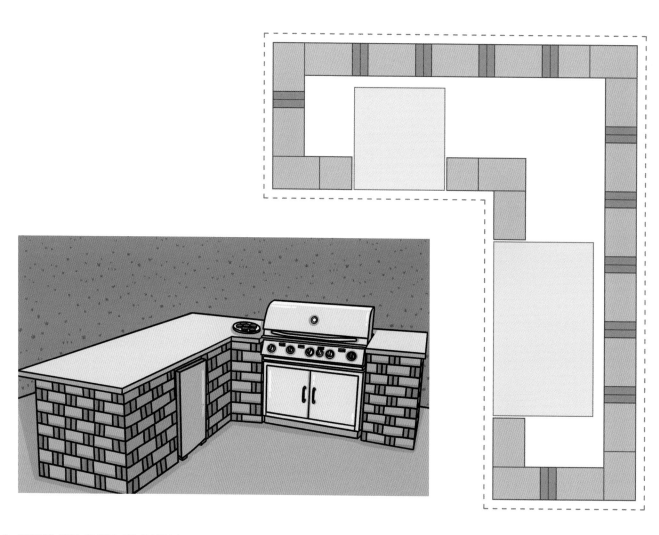

How to Build a Patio Kitchen

Measure, mark, and snap chalk lines for the kitchen footprint (use a framing square to check square in the corners). Tape off the outline using painter's tape and plastic sheeting, including taping the insets to mark refrigerator and grill placement. (This will protect the rest of the patio surface from mortar spillover.)

Set all the corner pavers in place and use a long, clear 2 × 4 and a 4' level to check the patio drainage slope. Raise the 2 × 4 to determine the distance of adjustment you'll need to make in laying the base, so that the countertop is level. Check level both ways.

Mix quick-set concrete to a consistency that holds together but is not overly dry or wet. Set the corner blocks at the appropriate heights. Check for level and tap any stone sitting too high with the trowel handle or a mallet.

As soon as the corner block concrete bases are set and cured, create a ½"-thick bed of concrete, as wide as a paver, running between two corner blocks. You can use a trowel, but a flat shovel or spade will be quicker. Leave gaps for the refrigerator and grill, unless either or both is meant to be mounted on a lip of pavers (many outdoor gas ranges are designed for this type of installation).

(continued)

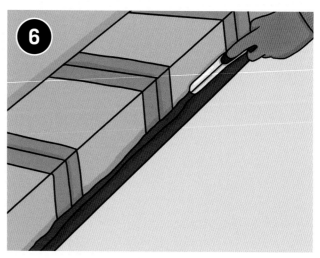

Following the pattern for the pavers you're using, set the pavers in the concrete bed for the first row. Check level and adjust as you go (check front to back and side to side). Add concrete under any that are low, and tap down any that are too high.

Lay all the base pavers in the outline of the kitchen. Check that all are securely seated in the mortar. Check level one last time and adjust as needed. Remove a small paver in the pattern to allow access for the refrigerator power cord. Once the mortar bed is "thumbprint hard," smooth the edges with a jointing tool.

Remove the painter's tape and plastic, being careful not to disturb the mortar. Let the base fully cure for at least 1 hour (much longer in humid or wet weather) or according to the manufacturer's instructions. Clip the tip of the construction adhesive tube and put it into the caulk gun. Dot the top of the paver base to begin a new course of pavers.

Lay the second course of pavers in place on the base, following the pattern diagram for your pavers. Continue laying courses until you reach the top. Once the construction adhesive has cured, slide the refrigerator and grill into place.

How to Cast a Concrete Countertop

TOOLS + MATERIALS

Tape measure
Carpenter's pencil
(2) 8 × 4' × ¾"
   melamine white
   panel

Table saw or
   circular saw
Drill and bits
Paddle bit
Painter's tape
Silicone caulk

Caulk gun
Latex gloves
Quick-setting
   countertop
   concrete mix
   (base white)

Rubber mallet
6-mil plastic sheeting
120-grit sandpaper
Acrylic concrete
   sealant

Small fine-nap roller
   or foam roller
5-gallon bucket

Carefully measure and mark outlines for the two countertop sections on a sheet of melamine white panel (melamine-lined particle board). Use a carpenter's square to ensure all corners are square. Cut 2" wide strips of melamine from the second sheet, matching the length of each outline section. Use a fine-tooth plywood-cutting blade and cut on the outside of the marked line. Take your time and cut carefully because all the form sides must be exactly the same width.

Drill countersunk pilot holes in the edges of the form sides (to prevent them from splitting), and screw each form side to its proper location using ½" deck screws.

(continued)

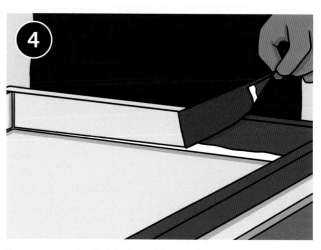

Thoroughly clean the form bed and sides. Carefully line both sides of the seams between sides and bed with painter's tape, leaving about 1/16" between tape and seam on both the bed and sides. Spread a thin bead of silicone caulk along the seams. Smooth each bead—removing caulk as needed—with a fingertip dipped in water.

As soon as you're finished applying caulk, remove the tape along the seams. Allow the caulk to dry completely. Line the top of the form sides with painter's tape

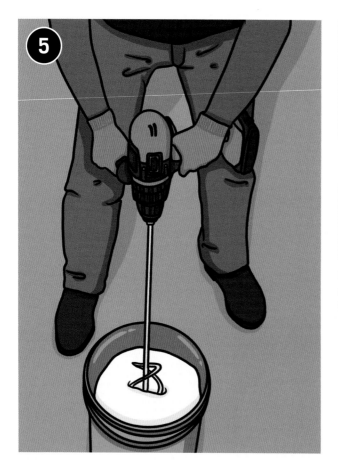

Fill the mold with concrete halfway up the sides. Smooth the surface with a grout float. Lay rebar (or steel mesh for smaller countertops) crisscrossed on the surface of this first layer.

Mix the countertop concrete using a 5-gallon bucket and a drill with a paddle attachment. Add white colorant (or the color you prefer; you can also leave it natural) and mix the concrete thoroughly. Pour the concrete into the mold. *Note: Depending on the size of your countertop, you may need a barrel mixer to mix the proper quantity of concrete. You can also tint the base white by adding concrete tint to the water before mixing.*

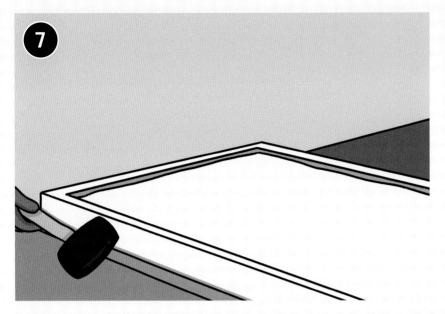

Fill the mold the rest of the way. Screed the top with a straight 2 × 4. Repeat in both directions at least 3 times. Tap the form sides with a rubber mallet to release air bubbles and ensure the mix is consolidated.

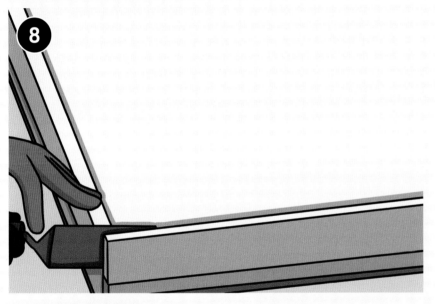

Cover the concrete with plastic sheet and leave undisturbed for 24 hours, or the time recommended on the concrete bag. Unscrew and pry off the form sides. Flip the counter with the assistance of a helper and inspect the top surface of your countertop. *Note: If there are noticeable gaps in the top, you can fill them with nonsanded acrylic tile grout in a matching tint. Mix the grout to a slurry and spread with a putty knife, let dry, and sand level with fine sanding paper.*

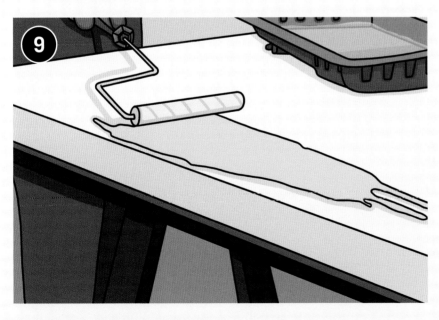

Sand the countertop, clean off the dust, and drape plastic over the top (it should be tented to avoid resting on the surface). Allow it to cure for an additional three days, then use a helper to move the countertop onto the top of the laid paver base. Check for proper positioning and roll with an acrylic concrete cure-and-seal product to seal the surface. Put the refrigerator and grill back in place if you removed them to place the countertop.

Patio Bar

A simple patio bar quickly becomes the centerpiece of outdoor entertaining and is the ideal way to take cookouts and outdoor gatherings to the next level. This basic structure isn't terribly difficult to master, but has several design features that makes it a joy to use, regardless of which side of the bar you're on.

The greatest challenge in building this patio entertainment feature is being precise with all measurements. Beyond that, the design is adaptable and forgiving of abuse. It has been made even simpler thanks to a lack of plumbed or wired features. However, it's simple enough to add either of those with an extension cord from an outdoor outlet, or plumbing tied into the house system. For maximum portability, you may want to add casters to the bottom frame (but make sure at least two are locking casters).

We've spec'd the project to use pressure-treated wood for the frame with cedar cladding. This ensures the bar will last a decade or more, even left out in the elements in an unshaded spot.

TOOLS + MATERIALS

Tape measure
Carpenter's pencil
Table saw or circular saw
Jig saw (optional)
Speed square
Drill and bits
Pocket jig (optional)
Bar clamps
3" deck screws
2" deck screws

1" stainless steel wood screws
1½" brads
Claw hammer
Torpedo level
Leveling furniture glides
Waterproofing sealant, stain, or paint (optional)
Brush (optional)

PATIO BAR PLANS

Frame side view

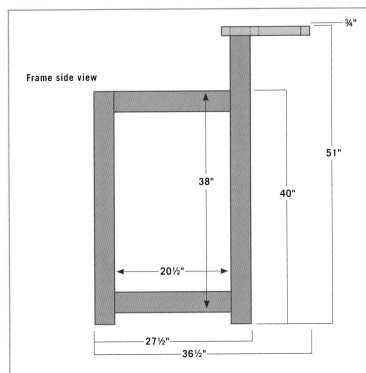

¾"

51"

38"

40"

20½"

27½"

36½"

Frame front view

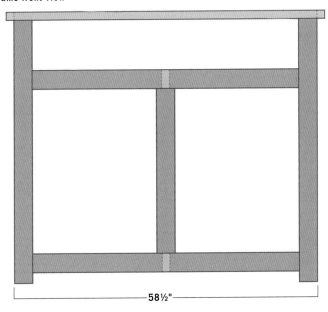

58½"

Top ledge frame

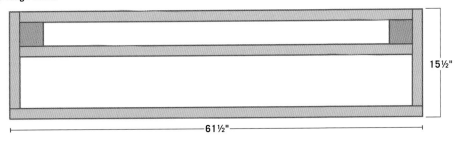

15½"

61½"

CUT LIST

Base frame legs, rear: (2) 4 × 4 × 40" pressure-treated pine

Base frame legs, front: (2) 4 × 4 × 51½" pressure-treated pine

Base frame side rails: (4) 2 × 4 × 20½" pressure-treated pine

Base frame f & b rails: (2) 2 × 4 × 51½" pressure-treated pine

Base frame vertical braces: (2) 2 × 4 × 31" pressure-treated pine

Base frame horizontal braces: (2) 2 × 4 × 31" pressure-treated pine

Ledge frame rails: (2) 2 × 2 × 58½" cedar

Ledge frame fascia: (1) 2 × 2 × 61½" cedar

Ledge frame sides: (2) 2 × 2 × 14" cedar

Countertop & bottom: (2) ½ × 27½ × 58 ½ " birch plywood (or exterior pressure-treated if painting)

Side cladding: (14) 1 × 6" × 27½" cedar

Front cladding: (7) 1 × 6 × 60" cedar

Interior shelf cleats: (2) 2 × 2 × 20½" pressure-treated pine

Interior shelf slats: (7) 2 × 4 × 58½" pressure-treated pine

Ledge shelf: (4) 1 × 4 × 61½" cedar

How to Build a Patio Bar

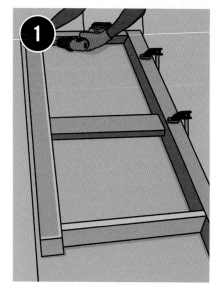

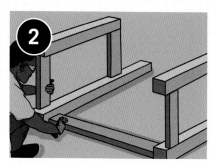

Cut all the lumber to the cut list dimensions. Clamp one front and one rear frame leg to a work surface. Position the side rails: one flush with the shorter leg end on one end (and 11" down from the end of the longer, front leg), and one 2" in from the opposite ends on of the legs. Check for square on both sides with a speed square. Screw the rails to the legs with 3" decks screws driven toenail fashion. Repeat with the remaining two legs and side rails.

Lay both leg pairs, parallel to one another, on the front (longer leg) face. Measure up 2" from the bottom end and use 3" deck screws screw the bottom front rail to the legs on both sides, toenail style. Repeat with the top rail, aligning it to match the side top rails. Repeat with the top and bottom back rails, between the shorter legs.

Measure, mark, and drill countersunk holes centered on the bottom of each leg, for the leveling feet. Use a hammer to tap in the anchor, and thread in the foot for each leg.

Stand the frame right-side up. Screw the rear top and bottom rails to the legs, aligned with the other rails. Measure the center point of the front and back bottom rails, for the placement of the horizontal brace. Position, check for square, and screw each the brace in place, toenail fashion. Repeat for the top brace. Install the vertical braces in the same way.

Use a speed square to mark the 3½" × 3½" corner cuts for the top countertop on either side of the long edge. Mark the bottom with the corner cuts on every corner, and 1½" × 3½" notches for the front and back center posts. Make the corner cuts with a circular saw or jig saw. Check fit, adjust as necessary, and then drill countersunk pilot holes and screw the surfaces in place to the legs and rails with 3" deck screws.

Carefully measure and mark 18" up from the leg bottoms, on the inside of the frame. Align and clamp the shelf cleats on each side on these marks. Drill pilot holes and screw the cleats to the legs with 3" deck screws.

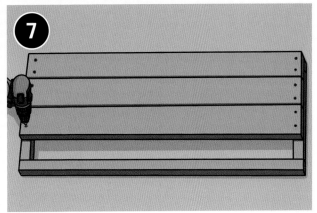

Build the outer ledge frame by drilling pilot holes and screwing the ledge frame sides to the longer front and back pieces (check the corners with a speed square to ensure the frame is square). Dry lay the ledge top boards in place. Lightly sand the board ends as necessary for a neat appearance, and then drill pilot holes and nail the boards to the frame all around with brads. Use a nailset to sink the brads

Fasten the inner ledge support rail to the front (bar stool side) of the front legs, flush with outsides and the tops of the legs. Drill and countersink pilot holes, and fasten the ledge frame to the legs and support rail ends with 3" decks screws.

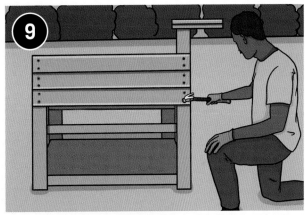

Start from one side of the bar frame and position the first cladding board flush to the top of the plywood countertop edge and front and back of the frame. Drill pilot holes and nail the board in place with brads. Align the second board underneath the first, and nail it in place. Repeat until you have completely covered the side.

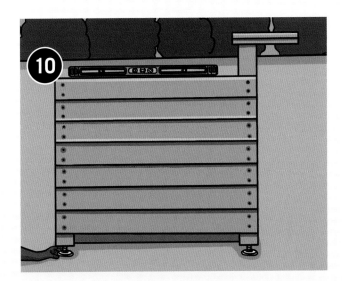

Repeat the process with the opposite side. Clad the front in the same way, making sure the boards are aligned on all sides. Seal, stain, or paint the bar and let it dry. Set in the final location and adjust the feet to level the bar front to back and side to side.

Patio Privacy-Screen Planter

Sometimes the view into your yard can be more concerning than the view from your patio. In those cases, where privacy becomes a priority, it's wise to use the occasion as an opportunity to add a showcase feature to your patio setting.

This privacy screen rewards some basic woodworking effort with three benefits: the construction is a handsome piece all by itself; the screen affords a sense of privacy and intimacy without blocking air flow; and the planter offers plenty of room for a wonderful flower, foliage, or edible garden right next to the patio.

This is designed to manageable dimensions and simple construction that makes it a great project even for someone with limited woodworking experience. You can even build multiples block off a longer patio edge.

Made of durable cedar, this will weather to a handsome gray if you leave it unfinished, or you can keep the "as new" appearance with clear waterproofing sealant. If you're finishing the unit,

do that before planting to avoid contaminating the soil. Lastly, the box is designed with feet to allow for drainage; you can add casters to make it more portable and movable as need dictates.

PATIO PRIVACY-SCREEN PLANTER

Planter Front and Back Frame

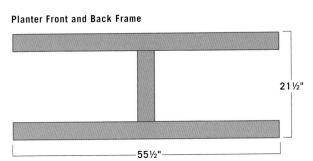

21½"

55½"

Planter Frame, Top View

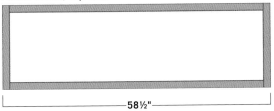

58½"

Cladding Frame Top View

Planter End Frame

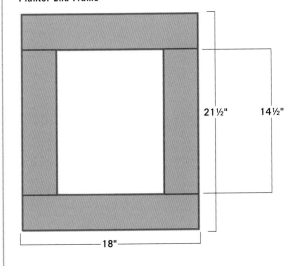

21½" 14½"

18"

CUT LIST

Frame f & b rails: (4) 2 × 4 × 55½" pressure-treated pine

Frame f & b supports: (2) 2 × 4 × 14½" pressure-treated pine

Frame end rails: (4) 2 × 4 × 18" pressure-treated pine

Frame end supports: (4) 2 × 4 × 14½" pressure-treated pine

Planter bottom: ½ × 58½ × 22" exterior-rated plywood

Planter cladding f & b: (8) 1 × 6 × 61½" cedar

Planter cladding sides: (8) 1 × 6 × 18" cedar

Trellis legs: (2) 5/4 × 4 × 70" cedar

Trellis cap: 5/4 × 4 × 66" cedar

Trellis cleats: (2) 2 × 2 × 48" cedar square baluster

Trellis: 48 × 60 diamond privacy cedar lattice panel (or vinyl)

Frame front cap: 1 × 4 × 64" cedar

Frame side caps: (2) 1 × 4 × 16½" cedar

Feet: (3) 2 × 4 × 18" pressure-treated pine

Trellis Frame

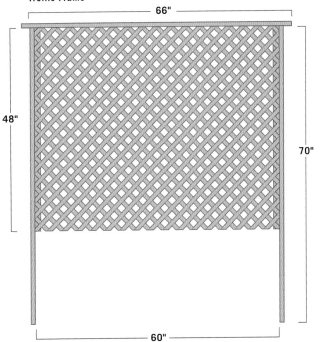

66"

48"

70"

60"

How to Build a Patio Privacy-Screen Planter

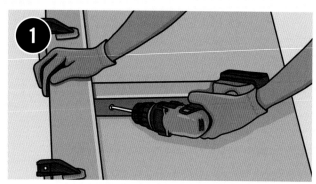

Cut all the lumber to the cut list dimensions. Clamp a front frame rail to the work surface. Center the support along the length of the rail. Drill angled pilot holes (toenail style) on each side of the support, into the rail. Screw the support to the rail with 3" deck screws. Clamp the second rail to the work surface and screw the support to the second rail in the same way. Repeat the process to construct the frame back

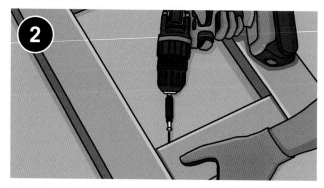

Construct an end assembly by clamping a corner at a time and driving 3" deck screws at each inside corner, through the shorter support into the rail. Repeat with the second end assembly.

Join the front and back to the end assemblies by screwing the front and back rails, toenail fashion, to the end rails. Check each corner with a speed square before driving screws all the way in, to ensure the frame box is kept in square.

Use 3" deck screws to fasten the plywood bottom to the frame. Measure and mark the bottom for the center foot placement. Clamp the foot and screw it to the bottom using 2" deck screws. Repeat with the remaining two feet, flush with either end. Drill a random pattern of ¹⁄₁₆" drain holes across the bottom.

Drill pilot holes and nail the end cladding in a column on each end, using brads. (The boards should be flush with the frame sides.) The bottom board should overlap the edge of the bottom. Fasten the front cladding boards in the same way, flush on each end with the ends of the side boards. Repeat with the back of the box.

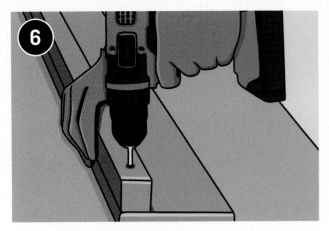

Clamp a trellis cleat in the corner of one trellis leg, following the length of the leg. Drill pilot holes and screw the cleat to the leg with 2" deck screws. Repeat with the second leg and cleat.

Lay the trellis legs on edge, with the cleats facing each other. Place the trellis in place resting on the cleats (measure that it's positioned correctly—longer side parallel to the planter box). Drill pilot holes and fasten the trellis to the cleats with 1" stainless steel wood screws.

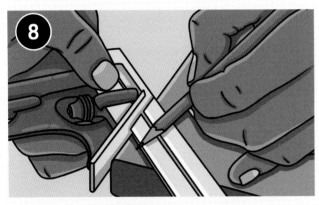

Use a speed square to mark both ends of the trellis cap with a 45° cut ¾" from the corners. Cut the corners with a circular saw. Center the top cap across the legs (there will be approximately 2¼" overhang on each end). Drill pilot holes and screw the top cap to the both legs.

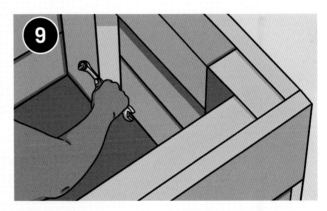

Stand the trellis assembly so that the legs are flush with the rear and bottom of the box. Drill ½" holes staggered every few inches up the leg and through the planter box frame. Bolt the trellis in place with carriage bolts, secured with a nut and washer on each.

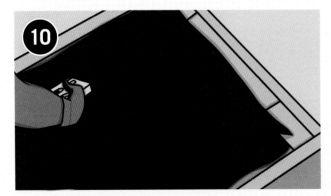

Staple landscape fabric to the inside of the planter, running up to and on top of the frame's top edges.

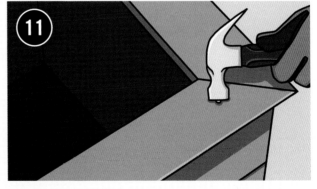

Cut the planter caps to a 45° angle (cut both ends of the front, and one end of each side cap). Move the trellis planter into its final position. Drill pilot holes and nail the caps to the frame with brads. Fill the planter with a base of gravel or rocks to ensure drainage, and then add soil and plants. Water thoroughly.

Conversion Charts

METRIC EQUIVALENT

Inches (in.)	1/64	1/32	1/25	1/16	1/8	1/4	3/8	2/5	1/2	5/8	3/4	7/8	1	2	3	4	5	6	7	8	9	10	11	12	36	39.4
Feet (ft.)																								1	3	3 1/12
Yards (yd.)																									1	1 1/12
Millimeters (mm)	0.40	0.79	1	1.59	3.18	6.35	9.53	10	12.7	15.9	19.1	22.2	25.4	50.8	76.2	101.6	127	152	178	203	229	254	279	305	914	1,000
Centimeters (cm)						0.95	1	1.27	1.59	1.91	2.22	2.54	5.08	7.62	10.16	12.7	15.2	17.8	20.3	22.9	25.4	27.9	30.5	91.4	100	
Meters (m)																							.30	.91	1.00	

CONVERTING MEASUREMENTS

TO CONVERT:	TO:	MULTIPLY BY:		TO CONVERT:	TO:	MULTIPLY BY:
Inches	Millimeters	25.4		Millimeters	Inches	0.039
Inches	Centimeters	2.54		Centimeters	Inches	0.394
Feet	Meters	0.305		Meters	Feet	3.28
Yards	Meters	0.914		Meters	Yards	1.09
Miles	Kilometers	1.609		Kilometers	Miles	0.621
Square inches	Square centimeters	6.45		Square centimeters	Square inches	0.155
Square feet	Square meters	0.093		Square meters	Square feet	10.8
Square yards	Square meters	0.836		Square meters	Square yards	1.2
Cubic inches	Cubic centimeters	16.4		Cubic centimeters	Cubic inches	0.061
Cubic feet	Cubic meters	0.0283		Cubic meters	Cubic feet	35.3
Cubic yards	Cubic meters	0.765		Cubic meters	Cubic yards	1.31
Pints (U.S.)	Liters	0.473 (Imp. 0.568)		Liters	Pints (U.S.)	2.114 (Imp. 1.76)
Quarts (U.S.)	Liters	0.946 (Imp. 1.136)		Liters	Quarts (U.S.)	1.057 (Imp. 0.88)
Gallons (U.S.)	Liters	3.785 (Imp. 4.546)		Liters	Gallons (U.S.)	0.264 (Imp. 0.22)
Ounces	Grams	28.4		Grams	Ounces	0.035
Pounds	Kilograms	0.454		Kilograms	Pounds	2.2
Tons	Metric tons	0.907		Metric tons	Tons	1.1

COUNTERBORE, SHANK + PILOT HOLE DIAMETERS

SCREW SIZE	COUNTERBORE DIAMETER FOR SCREW HEAD (IN INCHES)	CLEARANCE HOLE FOR SCREW SHANK (IN INCHES)	PILOT HOLE DIAMETER	
			HARD WOOD (IN INCHES)	SOFT WOOD (IN INCHES)
#1	.146 (9/64)	5/64	3/64	1/32
#2	1/4	3/32	3/64	1/32
#3	1/4	7/64	1/16	3/64
#4	1/4	1/8	1/16	3/64
#5	1/4	1/8	5/64	1/16
#6	5/16	9/64	3/32	5/64
#7	5/16	5/32	3/32	5/64
#8	3/8	11/64	1/8	3/32
#9	3/8	11/64	1/8	3/32
#10	3/8	3/16	1/8	7/64
#11	1/2	3/16	5/32	9/64
#12	1/2	7/32	9/64	1/8

NAILS

Nail lengths are identified by numbers from 4 to 60 followed by the letter "d," which stands for "penny." For general framing and repair work, use common or box nails. Common nails are best suited to framing work where strength is important. Box nails are smaller in diameter than common nails, which makes them easier to drive and less likely to split wood. Use box nails for light work and thin materials. Most common and box nails have a cement or vinyl coating that improves their holding power.

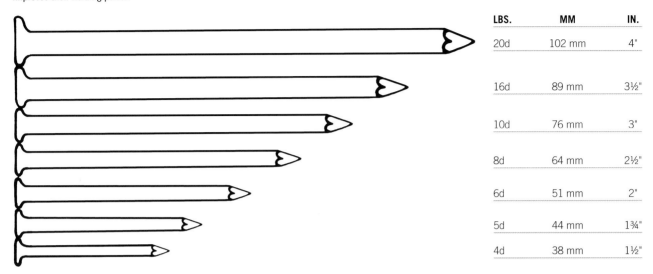

LBS.	MM	IN.
20d	102 mm	4"
16d	89 mm	3½"
10d	76 mm	3"
8d	64 mm	2½"
6d	51 mm	2"
5d	44 mm	1¾"
4d	38 mm	1½"

Resources

AZEK Building Products (page 132)
Composite permeable pavers
877-275-2935
www.azek.com

Belgard Hardscapes (page 62)
Pavers and retaining walls
877-235-4273
www.belgard.com

Black & Decker Corporation
Power tools & accessories
800-544-6986
www.blackanddecker.com

Borgert Products, Inc.
Concrete pavers and walls
800-622-4952
www.borgertproducts.com

Common Ground Alliance
"Call Before You Dig"
811
www.call811.com

Crossville Porcelain Tile
931-484-2110
www.crossvilleinc.com

Invisible Structures, Inc. (page 142)
Gravelpave® permeable subsurface grid
800-233-1510
www.invisiblestructures.com

Palram Americas (page 206)
Sunturf corrugated polycarbonate building panels and Palsun flat extruded polycarbonate sheeting
800-999-9459
www.palram.com

Porous Pave, Inc. (page 140)
Recycled rubber mulch and binder
888-448-3873
www.porouspaveinc.com

Quikrete
Cement & concrete projects
800-282-5828
www.quikrete.com

ScreenTight (page 220)
Porch screening systems
800-768-7325
www.screentight.com

ShadeSails.com (page 232)
Tensioned fabric canopies
956-772-4711
www.shadesails.com

Star Precast Concrete, LLC
(page 141)
Remanufactured glass pavers
970-989-5176
www.starprecast.com

Tenshon (page 232)
Shade sails
480-663-3166
www.tenshon.com

TERRECON, Inc. (page 138)
TERREWALKS® recycled plastic pavers
714-964-1400
www.terrecon.com

ZipUp Ceiling and Underdeck
(page 193)
Interjoist and underdeck ceiling systems
888-449-4787
www.zipupceilings.com

Photography Credits

Photo courtesy AZEK Building Projects, www.azekco.com, (877) 275-2935: pp. 124, 125 (all)

Photo courtesy Blinde, www.blindedesign.com, usa@blindedesign.com, (888) 590-3335: 21 (top)

Photo courtesy Borgert Products, www.bogertproducts.com, (800) 622-4952: pp. 69 (top)

Photo courtesy Chicago Specialty Gardens, Inc., www.chicagogardens.com, (773) 697-9897: pp. 112

Photo courtesy Crossville, www.crossvilleinc.com, (931) 484-2110: pp. 27

Photo courtesy Distinctive Designs: pp. 187 (bottom)

Dreamstime: pp. 25

Photo courtesy Ecosmart Fire, www.ecosmartfire.com, usa@ecosmartfire.com, (888) 611-7029: 40

Getty Images: pp. 29 (top), 138 top (© Allan Pollok-Morris)

Photo courtesy Tony Giammarino, www.tonygiammarino.com: pp. 69 (bottom right), 81

Photo courtesy Gibsons Recycling Depot, www.gibsonsrecycling.ca, (604) 740-1425: pp. 131 (bottom left)

Photo courtesy Heatscope, www.heatscopeheaters.com, usa@heatscopeheaters.com, (888) 850-4977: 16 (bottom)

Photo courtesy Huettl Landscape Architecture, www.huettldesign.com, (925) 937-6400: pp. 114 (bottom)

iStock: pp. 63, 131 (bottom right), 166, 179 (bottom two)

Khrystyna Khristianova: 113 (bottom) (Landscape Design by Yardzen)

Shelley Metcalf: pp. 33 (left), 104, 184 (William Bocken Architecture & Interior Design, Paul Adams Landscape Design)

Photo courtesy of O.W. Lee Co., Inc., www.owlee.com, info@owlee.com, (830) 267-9533: 10, 17, 20 (top), 23 (top)

Jerry Pavia: pp. 26 (right), 54, 80, 136, 138 (lower two), 160, 169 (bottom right), 179 (top two)

Photo courtesy Porous Pave, www.porouspaveinc.com, (888) 448-3873: pp.131 (middle right)

Sasha Reiko Photograph: 114 (top) (Landscape Design by Yardzen)

Photo courtesy Shademaker USA, shademakerusa.com, info@shademakerusa.com, (626) 338-8810: 19 (top)

Shutterstock: pp. 8, 23 (bottom), 24, 32,169 (bottom left),180, 181, 218

Photo courtesy of Texas Outdoor Lighting, texasoutdoorlighting.com, info@texasoutdoorlighting.com, (512) 504-3030: 19 (bottom), 20 (bottom), 21 (bottom), 33

Photo courtesy Treasure Garden, Inc., www.treasuregarden.com, info@treasuregarden.com, (626) 338-8810: pp. 6, 11, 28

Versa-LOK® Retaining Wall Systems/www.versa-lok.com: pp. 30

Photo courtesy of Yardzen, Inc., yardzen.com, (888) 927-3936: 22

Index

A

access, 12
acid staining, 29
arbors, 35, 38
area lights, 181
ashlar stone, 106
atmosphere, 12

B

bar, patio, 228–231
batterboards, 42
bleed water, 90
brick
    cutting, 59, 146
    edging, 50
    mortared, 76–79
    overview of, 24
    salvaged, 33
    sandset, 56–62, 142–147
building codes, 12

C

circular paver patio, 70–75
circular saws, 86
cladding posts, 211
climate control, 14–15
cobblestone paver patio, 63–69
cobblestones, 63
composite permeable pavers, 124–127
concrete
    coloring, 156
    coverage, 88
    decorative path, 154–157
    edging, 52–53
    evaluating surfaces of, 98
    finishing, 90
    next to a house, 92
    pavers, 25
    poured, 28–29, 88, 148–153
    round patio, 91–95
    slab patio, 88–95
    tiled, 96–103
control joints, cutting, 98
conversion charts, 236–237
crushed stone, 30–31
curves, 52–53, 60, 68, 101, 127, 140,
    142–143, 157
custom surfacing, 156

D

decomposed granite, 30
decorative concrete path, 154–157
design factors, 11
design themes
    alfresco at home, 16–17
    focus on fire, 20–21
    overhead structures, 18–19
    pool partners, 22–23
divided concrete slab, 29
doors, screen, 216–217
drainage, 13, 113, 116. See also
    permeable surfaces
drainpipes, 195
dray stone wall, 81

E

easements, 12
edging
    brick paver, 50
    concrete curb, 52–53
    configurations for, 50
    invisible, 49
    landscape timber, 54
    lumber, 55
    overview of, 48
    rigid paver, 48–49
    stone, 51
enclosures, 196–209
environmentally-friendly materials, 33
excavation, 42–47

F

fan-shaped pavers, 71
fire, focus on, 20–21
fire pits, 106–109
flagstone
    cutting, 87
    garden steps, 175–179
    overview of, 26
    sandset, 80–87
    walkway, 158–159
flood lights, 181
fountains, 35

G

granite, decomposed, 30
gravel, 161–165
gutters, 186–192

H

hardscaping basics, 9–39

K

kitchen, patio, 222–227

L

landscape steps, 141
landscape timbers
    edging, 54
    steps using, 170–174
layout, 10, 42
lighting, 20–21, 180–183
limestone blocks, 179
loose materials patio, 104–105
loose-fill patio with fire pit, 106–109
low-voltage lighting, 180–183
lumber edging, 55

M

materials
    climate control and, 15
    concrete pavers, 25
    decorative effects, 29
    environmentally-friendly, 33
    loose, 30–31, 104–105, 106–109, 160
    nature-friendly, 111–115, 124–131
    overview of, 24–33
    stone tile, 27
    See also brick; concrete; flagstone;
    stone; tile
mock-ups, 10
molds, 29, 154
mortared paver patio, 76–79

N

nature-friendly materials, 124–131
nature-friendly patios
    gallery of, 112–115
    overview of, 111

O

open grade drainage rock, 116
overhead structures, 18–19

P

paths. *See* walkways & paths
patio bar, 228–231

patio enclosures, 196–209
patio kitchen, 228–231
pavers
    choosing, 69
    circular, 70–75
    composite permeable, 124–127
    concrete, 25
    cutting, 59
    fan-shaped, 71
    interlocking, 62
    mortared, 76–79
    nature-friendly, 112–115
    patterns for, 61, 69
    recycled glass, 131
    recycled plastic, 130–131
    spaced masonry, 120–123
pea gravel, 30–31
pebbled stepping stone path, 166–169
perimeter trenches, 13
permeable subbases, 116–119
permeable surfaces, 115
planning, practical considerations for, 10–15
plans
    drawing, 34
    sample, 35–39
planter, privacy screen, 232–235
plants, 16, 85
pool partners, 22–23
porcelain tile, 32
poured concrete walkway, 148–153
privacy screen planter, 232–235

Q
quarry tile, 32

R
recycled glass patios, 131
recycled plastic pavers, 138–139
recycled rubber chips, 131
retaining walls, 36
river rock, 31
rubber chips, recycled, 131
rubber tile patio, 128–129
runoff, 13
runoff gutters, 193–195

S
saltillo tile, 32
sand-based soil, 85
sandset brick patio, 56–62
sandset brick walkway, 142–147
sandset flagstone patio, 80–87

screen doors, 226–227
screening systems, 210–217
seeded concrete, 29
setback restrictions, 12
shade sails, 218–221
shadows, 14
simple gravel path, 161–165
size, 10
sloping yards, 36
soil, 85
spaced masonry pavers, 120–123
spacer gauge, 162
spacers, using, 122
spine-based screening systems, 211
spotlights, 181
stacked slabs, 179
steppers
    choosing, 167
    concrete, 169
stepping stone paths, 140, 166–169
steps
    flagstone, 175–179
    landscape, 141
    timberframed, 170–174
stone
    about, 26–27
    ashlar, 106
    buying, 27
    crushed, 30–31
    cutting, 86–87
    dressing, 87
    edging, 51
    tile, 27
    trimming, 51
    walls, 81
    See also flagstone
subsurface grids, 132–135
sunlight, 14, 218–219
surfacing, custom, 156
swales, drainage, 13

T
task lighting, 21
terraces, 179
terra-cotta tile, 32
tile
    cutting curves in, 101
    porous, 103
    rubber, 128–129
    selecting, 32
tiled concrete slab, 96–103
timber garden steps, 170–174

timbers
    cutting, 172
    steps using, 170–174
tinting, 29
traffic routes, 10
trenches, 13

U
underdeck patio, 186–192
use considerations, 10
utilities, 12, 42

W
walkways & paths
    decorative concrete path, 154–157
    designing, 138
    flagstone, 158–159
    laying out, 139–141
    lighting for, 180–183
    overview of, 137
    pebbled stepping stone path, 166–169
    poured concrete walkway, 148–153
    reinforcing, 149
    sandset brick, 142–147
    simple gravel path, 161–165
    sloping, 149
    wheelbarrow, 118
walls, stone, 81
well lights, 181
wheelbarrow path, 118
wind currents, 15
wood chips, 31
wood edging, 55

Z
zoning laws, 12